EMBROIDERY
STUDIO

EMBROIDERY STUDIO

· THE ULTIMATE WORKSHOP ·
DESIGN, TECHNIQUE AND INSPIRATION

THE EMBROIDERERS' GUILD

PHOTOGRAPHS OF THE EMBROIDERERS' GUILD COLLECTION BY DUDLEY MOSS

David & Charles

(Page 2) *Detail of Syrian sleeve, one of a pair in the Embroiderers' Guild Collection. The embroidery is worked in counted thread techniques on evenweave linen*
EG no 1567; Syria; early twentieth century;
87 x 37cm (34¹/4 x 14¹/2in) (PHOTOGRAPHY: DUDLEY MOSS)

A DAVID & CHARLES BOOK
Copyright © EG Enterprises 1993, 1996
Stitch diagrams © David & Charles 1993, 1996
First published 1993
First paperback edition 1996

EG Enterprises has asserted its right to be identified as author of this work in accordance with the Copyright, Designs and Patents Act 1988.

A catalogue record for this book is available from the British Library.

ISBN 0 7153 0482 8

Typeset by ABM Typographics Ltd, Hull
and printed in Singapore by CS Graphics Pte Ltd
for David & Charles
Brunel House Newton Abbot Devon

CONTENTS

INTRODUCTION

The aim of *Embroidery Studio* is to demonstrate that in planning and designing an original piece, you can gain inspiration from studying historical textiles. A selection of embroideries from the Embroiderers' Guild Collection has been carefully chosen to provide a variety of starting points, using British and foreign examples, and ranging from sixteenth-century blackwork to the simple appliqué and stitching typical of the Needlework Development Scheme of the 1950s. Seeing how others have produced a totally individual piece by this means will, I hope, make your fingers itch to explore and experiment for yourself.

The contributors are all members of the Practical Study Group of the Embroiderers' Guild with a wide range of experience in teaching and as practising artists. Each has used her own specialised expertise to present an individual interpretation of her particular example, and in doing so explains and helps you to understand her thought processes.

Their research and the development of their ideas will provide the stimulus for you to experiment for yourself, play with your own new ideas, push forward the boundaries and discover new skills. For those of you who have only attempted simple embroidery until now, you will be guided along new paths and will have the ultimate satisfaction of creating original and exciting work.

Through the embroideries you will discover and explore traditional patterns and designs from countries as far apart as England, Russia and India, and how they can be changed to produce different effects. You will learn that simple stitches can be used to make intricate patterns, and also that our continuing fascination with the natural world will always provide rich source material, reassuring us that inspiration is never far away.

Enjoy *Embroidery Studio* and discover your own creativity.

Ann Joyce
Director, the Embroiderers' Guild

Drawing of Chinese woman's jacket
(DRAWING: MARY YOULES)

CHAPTER ONE

LIGHT AND SHADE

Amanda J. Clayton

ON FIRST seeing this piece of machine embroidery, I was surprised by its sophistication, considering it is dated 1938. The mat was designed by Rebecca Crompton and available information seems to suggest that it may have been executed by Dorothy Benson at the Singer Sewing Machine Company, although there is no evidence to confirm this.

Rebecca Crompton is considered to be a leader and innovator in producing fresh ideas in freedom of design; many of these are described in her book *Modern Design in Embroidery*, and her machine embroidery demonstrates considerable versatility and good contrast between the stitches. The stitches on this embroidery include crazy stitch (vermicelli), whip stitch, darning and eyelet holes and the mat is finished with a corded scalloped border with added decorative loops. The design consists of four women flanked by horses with a cutwork sun motif in the centre, decorated with machine-made needle-lace fillings and surrounded by a variety of floral patterns. The mat is worked mainly in neutral tones with some metal threads on a matching fine rayon organdie, making a sensitive and delicate finished work.

The embroidery is interesting for two reasons: it poses the question 'How far have we actually progressed in machine embroidery techniques since 1938?'; and it was thought to be an early piece of artwork rather than a functional practical mat.

Machine techniques have only recently been changed, or made easier, by sophisticated machines – although even a highly sophisticated machine will only produce good work if it is guided by a creative and inventive mind. The basic techniques already existed in 1938, with darning stitch being the basis of free machining. However, it was surprising to find, while researching, that most of the early examples of machine embroidery were made without a swing needle. Skilful control was therefore necessary when moving the frame in the machine to produce a varied width satin stitch.

There are many books which go into detail about machine embroidery, so the main emphasis here is on personal interpretations of this piece rather than its historical presence. The excitement of this work comes from its delicacy and fragility, the wonderful variations in line on a near-sheer fabric and the combination of hand- and machine-embroidery techniques.

My first step towards producing a contemporary piece inspired by this work was to compile a sketchbook incorporating Mrs Crompton's philosophy on drawing – especially in the use of line and the arrangement of tone and fillings when designing. The sketchbook work consisted of drawing, painting, written research, photography, photocopies – anything that was visual or appropriate to the way of thinking. Among the drawings in the sketchbook were some of a collection of shards picked up on a beach in Cornwall, and these were used as the design for the hanging.

The heavy stitching contrasted with the fragile background of Rebecca Crompton's piece were a strong influence on me. At the same time I was also influenced by some heavily decorated ecclesiastical embroideries seen in the Icon Museum at Paphos, Cyprus. Characteristics such as well-worn surfaces combined with repetitive couching, subtle trailing, delicate fillings, and the contrast of highly twisted thread over floss fibre gave a basis for technique.

Sketchbook pages from Icon Museum, Cyprus, and stitch samples related to them
(DRAWING: AMANDA CLAYTON. PHOTOGRAPHY: DAWN ROBERTSON)

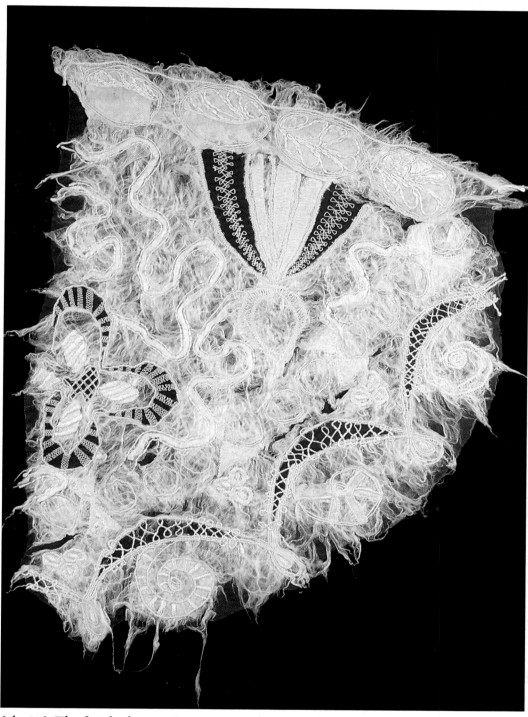

(opposite) *Mat of white rayon organdie with machine embroidery in white cotton and silver threads. Cutwork circles with needlemade fillings and a scalloped border with detached loops. The design is of women flanked by horses with a sun motif in the centre. Designed and made by Rebecca Crompton EG no 1046; 1938; 40.5 x 38cm (16 x 15in); given by the Needlework Development Scheme*

(PHOTOGRAPHY: DUDLEY MOSS)

(above) *The finished contemporary piece. Felted paper made from linen fibre with silk thread for hand-stitching. Designed and worked by Amanda Clayton*

(PHOTOGRAPHY: DAWN ROBERTSON)

(above) *Photographs and drawings of a collection of shards*

(DRAWINGS: AMANDA CLAYTON. PHOTOGRAPHY: DAWN ROBERTSON)

The monochrome colour scheme of the original also had a considerable influence. Although it is worked in neutral tones, it still has a strength of design and workmanship which might have been lost if worked in colour. This, together with a personal interest in irregular hand-spun silks and untwisted yarns and natural fibres, led me to make a series of experiments constructing background fabrics to stitch into.

I have used felted paper as a background fabric for much of my recent work and it seemed a suitable medium for interpreting this particular piece. Felt is made from animal fibres, and paper from cellulose (vegetable), and felted paper is a combination of these constructed in a similar manner to felt.

It is a simple process and can be carried out with a minimum of equipment. Using a viscose cleaning cloth as a base, tease out and lay in one direction a thin layer of linen (flax) fibre. Place another layer at right angles to the first and a third layer in the same direction as the first. Cover with a second viscose cloth and wet thoroughly, but remove any excess water. Working on a stable wet surface, rub with a spoon in all directions for approximately ten minutes. The fibres swell and weaken when wet and the rubbing helps to break down the fibres so that they bind to each other, making a firm structure as the felted paper dries out.

This is the basic method for making felted paper, but interesting results occur by experimenting with the technique. Other types of similar fibre can be used instead of, or in conjunction with the linen. Wet the fibres with cold water, or with hot water and soap. Scraps of fabrics and threads or other materials could be trapped between the layers and it may be possible to add paper pulp during the making.

The final work was affected by my studies and various outside influences. The hanging is of felted paper made from linen fibre with hand-stitchery in silk thread using couching, herringbone, straight stitch and darning.

The neutral tones of white and cream were used to give the effect of light and shade combined with movement and texture, and the finished piece is designed to be a free-form hanging, displayed against the light to emphasise the ethereal quality.

Design pages from a sketchbook showing ideas that can be obtained for geometrical designs by working on square paper directly with a brush
(DRAWING: AMANDA CLAYTON. PHOTOGRAPHY: DAWN ROBERTSON)

CHAPTER TWO

GOLDEN STITCHES

Ann V. Sutton

THE ORIGINAL purpose of the sampler for needlewomen was as a 'treasured repository of stitches', but as pattern books became more widely available in the seventeenth century, its role as such diminished. As a result, in the following centuries, the hand of many a young girl became employed in the creation of band, cutwork, map and pictorial samplers. They became part of a girl's education and an exercise in neatness and perseverance.

The seventeenth-century spot sampler illustrated here would have been used as a reference sheet for patterns and so it is of great interest today. It is worked on a linen which has a count of 36 x 33 threads to the inch/2.5cm. It is pertinent to note that Irish linen was introduced into that country in 1633 by Thomas Wentworth, Earl of Stafford, the Lord Deputy for Ireland. This little sampler may be one of the first to have been stitched on such linen. Prior to this, most good quality linen used in Britain was imported from Egypt, France and Holland, as indicated by an entry in Edward VI's inventory of 1552 – a parchment book containing 'a sampler or set of patterns worked on Normandy canvas with green and black silks'.

This type of presentation is of more than passing interest to contemporary embroiderers, especially with the current popularity of paper-making. In Japan, simple yet wonderful books are made, some-

Story-board of drawings showing a collection of interlaced patterns

(DRAWING: ANN V. SUTTON. PHOTOGRAPHY: TIM BOWDEN)

A mid-seventeenth-century sampler in counted thread and canvaswork techniques. Worked on a linen ground fabric with a thread count of 36 x 33 threads to the inch/2.5cm, the embroidery has been worked in silk floss and gilt and silver-gilt metal threads.
EG no 1433; mid-seventeenth century; 15 x 26.5cm (6 x 10¹/₂in) (PHOTOGRAPHY: DUDLEY MOSS)

times stitched together or held by tapes or cords. When released the pages cascade from the cover or gently unpleat like a concertina, the tapes or cords keeping the structure or layout in place. A larger piece of work so constructed of many smaller sections would be transported easily, and quickly hung after being unfolded. Books about bookbinding, especially from the Orient, will provide stimulus and many starting-points for the embroidering paper-maker.

Floss silk as used on this spot sampler would have been imported from the Levant and brought to Britain by Venetian traders. It was both highly prized and highly priced, an ounce costing 2s–2s 6d in the sixteenth century; at that time it was called slave, sleave, or sleided silk. The stitches, worked in silk, rely on the counted thread, and they move between canvaswork and pulled work depending on the tension used by the stitcher. As the linen then was softer than contemporary canvas, there was no restriction in moving easily through different techniques, allowing them to co-exist happily rather than superimposing one on another.

Doubleback stitch is used to establish the framework of the grid patterns and these are filled with rice, rococo, knitting and cross stitches. The last of these, when pulled very tightly, give a more open effect; this aspect can be explored in modern work by contrasting the denseness of canvaswork with the laciness of pulled work.

The other threads used for stitching on the sampler are of gilt and silver-gilt metal. These were known as Venice, Cyprian or Damask gold and would have arrived from abroad in the same way as the silk. In most eras the use of metal thread was often restricted by the technical ability of the embroiderer, but not so with the needlewomen of the sixteenth century. They used many different lacings and interlacings, and variations of buttonhole stitch; all of which keep the thread working on the surface, not dragging it backwards and forwards through the background, a practice which often ends in disintegration of the thread. The stitches of earlier periods required a frame for ease of working, whereas the 'new' stitches of this period, such as buttonhole, chain, coral and plaited braid are more easily worked

in the hand. This is because late in the sixteenth century the needlewomen no longer relied on wire-drawn needles, but had good-tempered needles, which were necessary for working in this manner.

Many samplers of this type still exist in both public and private collections, and they are known as spot samplers because they are collections of scattered motifs without any formal sequence of arrangement. Repeating blocks of pattern, and motifs of figures, birds, animals and sprigs of flowers are frequently included, using the stitches previously mentioned as well as others such as plaited braid and raised chain band. Some of the designs would have been handed down through the generations and many more will have been added by inventive needlewomen engaged in their search for new and different motifs. An additional element expanding the scope of the sampler will have been the use of new or different kinds of threads as they became available. The apparent incompleteness of these samplers suggests that they were worked on intermittently, with new motifs and stitches added as the stitcher gained in expertise. They in fact reveal the entire working process used by the maker, and therefore provide considerable interest for present-day embroiderers.

Each time we look at the individual areas on the spot sampler it is easy to visualise the enthusiasm of

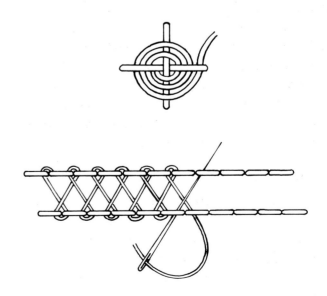

Threaded cross stitch (above), *and interlacing herringbone with back stitch*   (DRAWING: MOLLIE PICKEN)

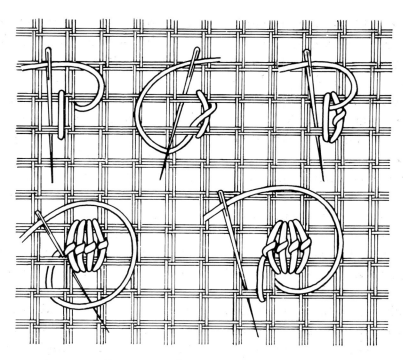

Rococo stitch (DRAWING: MOLLIE PICKEN)

the worker and to imagine hearing the words 'What can I try next? I wonder if this will work?' It was the possibility of displaying contemporary work in spot sampler form which provided the stimulus for the embroidery illustrated here.

One modern tool which had a hand in this work was the laser copier. A drawing was made of the interlacing on the dress worn by Mary Boleyn in a portrait dated 1567, and was translated by the copier into a 1 x 1mm ($^1/_{25}$ x $^1/_{25}$in) grid pattern. The fluid quality of the drawing disappeared, and a series of blocks and lines took its place. It was this visual alteration which provided the starting-point for the interlacing textile. Threaded cross stitch appears at the intersection of many of the patterns in the spot sampler, and it is used together with interlacing stitch on the contemporary sampler. Not only has threaded cross stitch been used with a variety of metal threads, but the intrinsic pattern created by its use has also been exploited.

Today, with so many various materials available at our fingertips, many individual surfaces can be created; numerous layers of different materials can be bonded, dyed, machine-embroidered, manipulated, patched, pieced and coloured. However, it is important to remember that a background is pre-

pared as a basis for stitching, and not to let it become the dominant feature overpowering the embroidery.

Had the early seventeenth-century embroideress had access to fabric paints, dyes, bonding agents and soluble fabrics, she would surely not have rested until she had explored many of the avenues that their use suggested. A combination of new materials and tools, hints from history, and the construction of specific backgrounds has resulted in this modern sampler. The gate has been opened, a journey started; where it will lead is but another avenue of exploration.

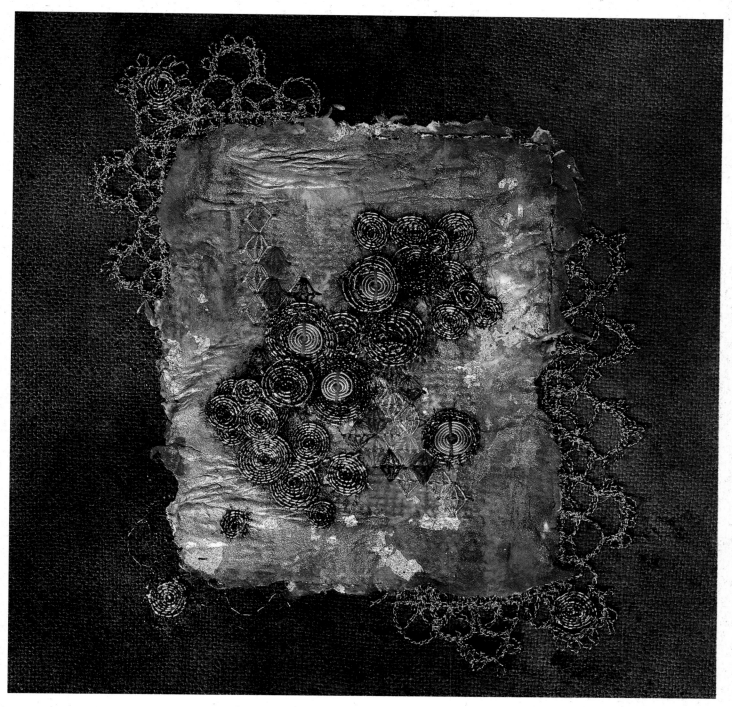

(opposite) *A form of modern sampler showing experimental stitching, inspired by the seventeenth-century spot sampler. Designed and worked by Ann V. Sutton* (PHOTOGRAPHY: TIM BOWDEN)

(above) *A small embroidery developed from the previous studies, using machine-couched gold thread, on a background of canvas and handmade paper, edged with machine-made lace. Designed and worked by Ann V. Sutton* (PHOTOGRAPHY: TIM BOWDEN)

CHAPTER THREE

A MAN'S WAISTCOAT

Sheila Miller

THE WAISTCOAT illustrated is typical of those made in England and other European countries at the end of the eighteenth and the beginning of the nineteenth centuries, its embroidery being the product of a professional workshop. It measures 74cm (25in), a shorter length style which became fashionable around 1780, earlier waistcoats being considerably longer and fuller, extending to the thighs.

Its cutaway front and elaborately embroidered decoration indicate that it was probably part of a dress suit, made for evening attire or for formal occasions, and would have been worn underneath a coat. For every day, straight-cut single or double-breasted waistcoats, often with a shawl collar and slit pockets, were more fashionable.

The waistcoat is made of fine ribbed cream silk, lined with white linen, and faced with a fine silk twill. The flaps on the shallow pockets are stitched down for about 2½cm (1in) at each side, possibly for security. Eight silk-embroidered buttons are attached from the neck to the cutaway front, but there are only five buttonholes and this gives the appearance of a V-shape when fastened, allowing for the shirt ruffles to be shown. It is interesting to note that the design made allowance for buttonholes, which were rather coarsely stitched over a gimp, across the embroidery before cutting.

The embroidery is worked in floss silks, in rose red, pale pink, rust, straw yellow, pale brown, sap green and pale veridian. Silver passing thread, purls and spangles are also used. The design consists of large sprays of stylised flowers with spangled stems merging into a ribbon of leaves which entwine a half-circle of silver spiky grass-like shapes. Narrower continuous motifs edge the stand-up collar and decorate the pocket flaps. Tiny sprays of flowers and leaves, highlighted with spangles, form a light powdering pattern on the front panels.

The waistcoat is finished with a narrow braid-like geometric pattern formed by satin-stitched triangular blocks, highlighted with spangles and edged with a silk gimp and silver purls worked to resemble a cord.

The garment is in very good condition although some of the spangles and accompanying stitches are missing, revealing the printed pattern underneath. Some indication of the delicate original colours can be seen on the back edge of the side panels, which would have been covered by the coat, and which may have been protected by being folded in storage.

Satin stitch is used throughout the embroidery. It was worked without any previous padding or outlining, and the thread is carried underneath the fabric as well as across its surface. This method gives a better tension, a smoother stronger stitch, and therefore wears longer than surface satin stitch which is worked almost entirely across the top of the fabric, and is sometimes used for economical reasons.

The petals are worked in bands of satin stitch in coloured floss and silver passing thread. At the base of the flower motifs the long spiky leaf shapes are embroidered in a diagonal satin stitch using silver passing thread, and the small leaf shapes are worked in silk floss. The sprig motifs are worked in a similar manner and the small stems are worked in silk outline stitch.

Passing thread consists of a very fine metal wire wound around a silk or nylon core which, because of its fineness and construction, is suitable for use as a sewing thread. To avoid damaging the fabric, a length of metal, about 5cm (2in), should be unravelled from the core, before it is threaded through the needle. A similar length of metal is stripped from the

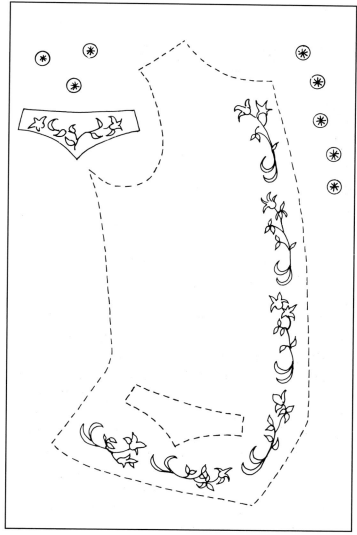

Part of a waistcoat 'shape' including buttons and a pocket tacked and embroidered on a length of fabric. The width of eighteenth-century silk was quite narrow, 19–21in (48–53cm) depending on where it was woven.

Method of securing spangles with purls:

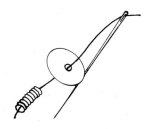

a) Needle threaded first with a purl and then a spangle so that the purl lies on the top of the spangle

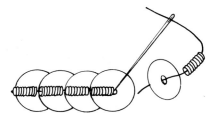

b) In subsequent stitches, the spangle is threaded onto the needle first, the purl covering the previous spangle

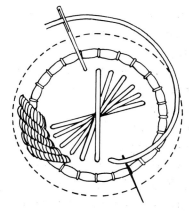

c) Partly worked button showing couched gimp overlaid with purls. The straight stitch decoration in the centre was finally neatened with a spangle

d) Satin stitch used as block shading

(DRAWINGS: SHEILA MILLER. STITCH DIAGRAMS: MOLLIE PICKEN)

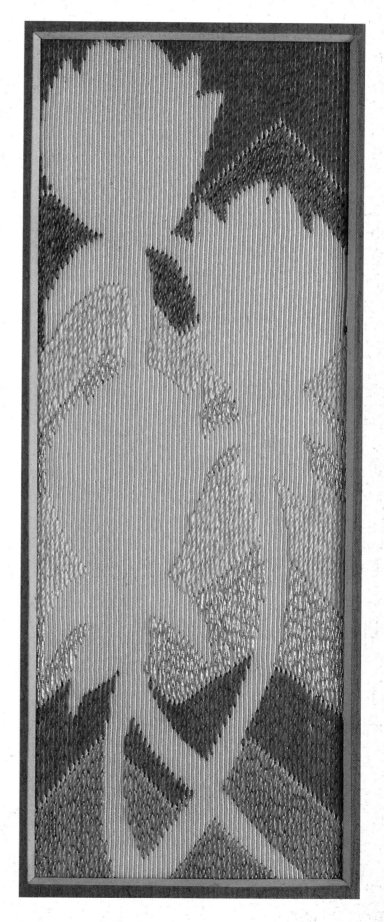

(opposite) *A man's waistcoat typical of those made both in England and on the Continent at the end of the eighteenth and the beginning of the nineteenth centuries. It is made of fine ribbed cream silk, lined with white linen, and the embroidery is worked in floss silks and silver passing thread with added purls and spangles EG no 124 1982; c1800; length 64cm (25in)*
(PHOTOGRAPHY: DUDLEY MOSS)

(above) *A detail showing stitchery and buttons*
(PHOTOGRAPHY: DUDLEY MOSS)

(right) *The completed panel. A ribbed silk background fabric was embroidered in chevron bands, stitching along the grooves of the fabric in split stitch, using silver thread and similar colours to the original. The flower shapes were left unworked to reveal the ribbed silk. Designed and worked by Sheila Miller*
(PHOTOGRAPHY: JIM PASCOE)

other end of the thread, and it is used to make a starting stitch a little distance away from the commencement of the work.

Metal embroidery threads were produced by the Gold and Silvery Wyredrawers who became a London Guild upon the granting of a charter in 1623. The thread, an expensive commodity, was supplied by Gold and Silvery Lacemen, who would buy back unwanted or undamaged thread from embroiderers for melting and re-use. This practice led to the craze for 'drizzling' amongst ladies of fashion who unpicked gold and silver lace and embroideries for pin money, resulting in the loss of many precious samples.

A lovely feature of the waistcoat is the flowing line of the stems on the larger sprays, formed by silver spangles attached to the fabric by silver purls. Metal purl consists of a coiled wire resembling a fine spring, and is used in embroidery in a similar way to

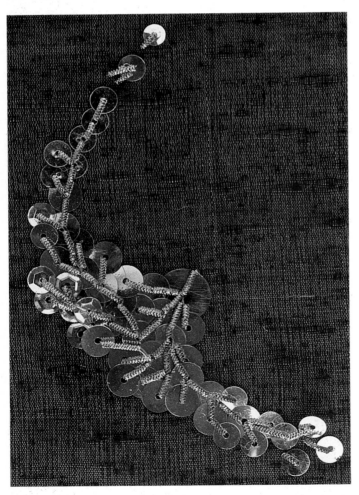

Sample showing a texture created by attaching spangles with cut rough purl (PHOTOGRAPHY: JIM PASCOE)

beading, the wire being cut into tiny lengths, each threaded with a waxed thread and then attached to the fabric.

The 'corded' edges of the waistcoat and buttons have been formed by sewing purls over a silk gimp in order to give a slightly raised effect. The star-shaped motif on each button is formed by working diagonal stitches in floss silk in an anticlockwise direction across a circular shape, and the centre is neatened with a spangle.

Although some professional embroiderers of the eighteenth century may have produced their own designs, most originated in the workshops of the pattern drawer who also supplied designs for amateur embroiderers. The design was transferred to the fabric by the 'prick and pounce' method.

The completed embroidery would be delivered as one piece of fabric, the 'shapes' remaining uncut, either directly to a customer, or to a retailer (perhaps a laceman, a mercer, a hosier, hatter or haberdasher). The waistcoat would be made up by the purchaser's tailor, who would be able to make any adjustments to the fit while shaping the back.

Abstracting a contemporary design from an historical source can produce difficulties, as the attraction of the original must be the reason for its choice as an inspiration. The design may well seem perfect in itself, and therefore difficult either to improve or re-create. Making a detailed copy may only produce a lifeless result, a dilution of another's idea. The contemporary translation, however, should reflect some elements in the design to link it with the original.

Inspiration may come from the techniques used, the colours, the inter-relation of form, background fabric, or perhaps in its use of a favourite theme. Any of these elements could be abstracted and used to create a contemporary embroidery.

The techniques used in the embroidered waistcoat are particularly satisfying. The coloured silk and silver chevron bands on the flower-heads form a contrast, as do the smooth spangles stitched down with purls which form the stems; and the textural contrast of spangles and purls could be used in metal-thread embroidery.

The predominant feature of the waistcoat design is the large floral sprays and it was from these that the

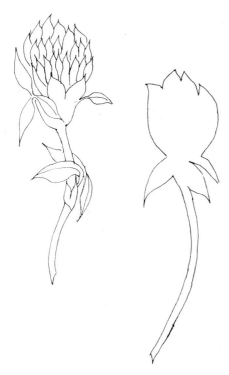

(above) *Stylised clover shapes cut out of tracing paper and tacked to the background fabric. Lines of tacking stitches were afterwards sewn across the panel to use as guidelines for the chevron background stitching*
(PHOTOGRAPHY: JIM PASCOE)

(right) *Partly worked panel showing guideline tacking*
(PHOTOGRAPHY: JIM PASCOE)

contemporary panel was designed. Because the flowers are stylised, it was difficult to decide on their natural origin. The shape of the heads and the chevron pattern are, however, reminiscent of a clover, and I decided to use this flower in my design.

A drawing was made of a clover, and re-drawn into a stylised floral shape. Using tracing paper, the shape was repeated, turned and overlapped until a satisfying design was made. A ribbed silk, similar to that of the waistcoat, was obtained for the background fabric. I decided not to embroider the flower shapes as this would too closely resemble the original, and instead the background fabric was embroidered in chevron bands, stitching along the grooves of the fabric in split stitch, using silver thread and silks in similar colours to the original. The flower shapes were left untouched, revealing the beautiful texture of the ribbed silk.

CHAPTER FOUR

ENCHANTED GARDENS

Jeanette Durrant

THE EARLY eighteenth-century bed-hanging illustrated is a bold confident piece of embroidery, bringing together all the best of the Englishwoman's skill with the needle, and her love and knowledge of gardening and herbs. The style of the design, with its Baroque curves and complete organic trees, indicates that the hanging was made towards the end of the fashion for large crewelwork hangings, c1700. It is worked in hand-spun vegetable-dyed wool on a twill weave fabric with linen warp and cotton weft, and this gives a firm support to the threads while being pliable and easy to stitch. The great variety of stitches and fillings, and the scale of the piece, indicate that it is almost certainly the work of professionals.

Hand-spun crewel wool of the time has a sheen and firmness which is used to good effect on the mound, where the richly textured stitches are packed closely together to make a solid base. The colours in the hanging have held remarkably well, especially the greens, and could have been dyed by professional dyers. The wool was coloured with vegetable dyes using a limited palette of yellow, blue and madder red, giving a softness and unity to the piece. Greens were made by overdyeing blue with yellow, and the shades and tints by using the same

Crewelwork hanging, part of an English bed-set. The embroidery is worked in vegetable-dyed crewel wool on a cotton/linen twill fabric. Two undulating tall trees with large curling leaves grow from a hillock, and smaller leaves, nuts and fruit fill the remaining spaces together with a squirrel, parrot and exotic bird. The heraldic beasts on the mound are a griffin, cockatrice and lion. A hare and rabbit feed on plants and flowers EG no 1282; c1700; 242 x 110cm (95 x 43¹/₄in); given by Mrs St O. Woods (PHOTOGRAPHY: DUDLEY MOSS)

dye several times until the colour was gradually exhausted.

The single motif of semi-naturalistic trees, growing from a hillock and filling the whole curtain, instead of a repeated pattern or mixture of images, is another indication of the date it was made. Late seventeenth-century and early eighteenth-century crewelwork designs were influenced by the fashion for Chinoiserie and the eastern Tree of Life designs. The ogee structure of the trunks on this example allows the leaves and small shapes to be developed individually, yet to retain a unity.

The main stitches on the leaves are cretan and stem stitch, with open fillings where the leaves curl. An interesting variety of edges helps to define the leaf shapes and soften the outline. In some areas the two-ply wool has been divided and worked in split stitch to obtain fine detail on fruits and animals. A professional pattern drawer would probably have printed the design onto the background fabric. The embroidery would have been worked with the fabric stretched on a frame.

Early crewelwork embroidery was worked mainly in monochrome using red, blue or black

Detail of leaf with fillings. Baroque curling leaf with solid areas in shaded stem and split stitch, edged with an arrowtail outline. The fillings are alternate rows of fishbone sprigs and wheatear. A smaller leaf has laidwork filling couched down with shaded cross stitch
(PHOTOGRAPHY: DUDLEY MOSS)

threads with enlarged scrolling designs of repeat motifs of flowers, fruits and insects previously found on costume. Some birds and insects were well established symbols and puns, and motifs such as the parrot, the strawberry and the potato flower were used simply because they were new and exotic.

Printed books with clear woodcut or engraved illustrations continued to be used as inspiration, as well as pattern books printed especially for the embroiderer. Favourites were *Gerard's Herbal* (1597), Gesner's *Historia Animalium* (1560), and later John Overton's *A New Booke of all Sortes of Beastes* (1660). Designs were copied directly from the books, which may explain the mix of scale and the odd juxtaposition of creatures and flora.

Another major influence came from the East. Europe had long been fascinated by tales of China

CREWELWORK STITCHES

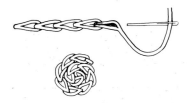

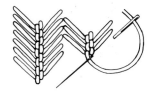

a) Split: *The needle steps back into the last stitch splitting the thread. Best worked using a soft thread or two-ply*

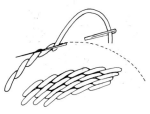

b) Stem: *Worked from left to right with the thread below the needle. For shaded fillings, follow the outline of the stitch*

c) Satin: *Short areas can be worked in blocks, keeping stitches close together and an even length*

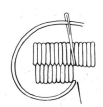

d) Satin encroaching: *Useful for shading. The second and subsequent rows of stitches enter between the base of the two stitches above*

e) Cretan: *Can be worked as a line or filling. Begin with a short centre stitch. Worked from left then the right making a plait down the centre. Can be worked close together or wide apart*

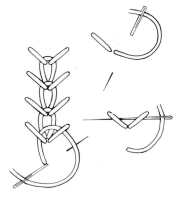

f) Wheatear: *From A, work two diagonal stitches at B and C. Enter again at A and bring the needle out below at D. Pass the needle under the two straight stitches above without entering the fabric*

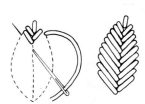

g) Fishbone: *Start with a small diagonal stitch. Insert at A and carry across to B. Then down to C and D*

Edging Stitches

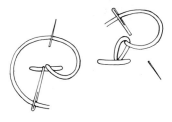

h) Petal: *Starting at A, work a back stitch to B coming out halfway back at C. Work a chain stitch to the side returning further down the line at D. The next 'stem' stitch should return to the base of the petal at C*

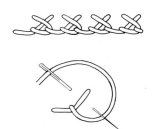

i) Crossed: *A version of buttonhole stitch with upright arms worked at angles to form a cross*

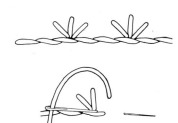

j) Arrowtail: *Work three stem stitches coming out at A. Make three small straight stitches returning into A. Repeat three stem stitches*

Mound Stitches

k) French knot: *Hold the thread taut while twisting it around the needle two times. Turn the needle completely and re-enter the fabric where it emerged. Slide the thread down the needle and hold with your other thumb until knot is complete.*

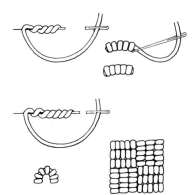

l) Bullion knot: *Use a firm thread and thick needle with a small eye. Pick up a small amount of fabric A to B and wrap enough coils round the needle to equal the space between A to B. Push coils down to eye of needle and hold in place with your thumb, returning the needle point through B*
Blocks of bullion are known as point rose

m) Basket stitch:
Stitches worked in alternate groups of vertical and horizontal satin stitch

n) Brick stitch: *Work first row in long and short satin stitch. Work following rows in even length satin stitch, first higher then lower than the last. Rows can be gradually shaded*

FILLING STITCHES

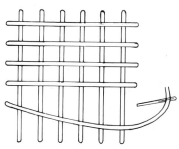

a) Basic grid: *Start at A. Enter at B and pick up grid width at C. Continue vertically to the end of the shape. Turn and work horizontally down the shape*

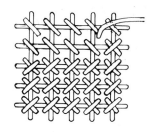

b) Cross stitch couching: *Couch grid down with rows of diagonal stitches, returning in the opposite direction. Can be shaded*

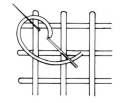

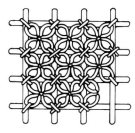

c) Chain stitch couching: *Using a wider grid, start in the centre of the square at A and make a diagonal chain stitch holding down the grid at C and returning to the centre. Continue zig-zagging to the end of the row. Turn and work in the opposite direction, couching down the grid intersections above*

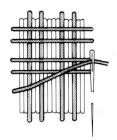

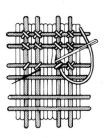

d) Laidwork over surface satin stitch: *Work a base of surface satin stitch. Lay a grid over the satin stitch in another colour. Couch down grid with cross stitch where the grid intersects*

Filling variations: *Work a wide grid.*

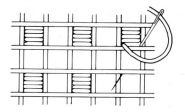

Fill in with satin stitch blocks.

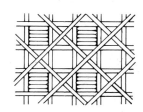

Work diagonal grid over the blocks using another colour.

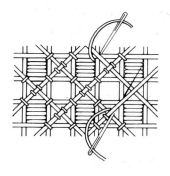

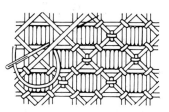

Couch down diagonal lines in sequence
(DRAWINGS: MOLLIE PICKEN)

and the Orient, told by merchants returning with silks, porcelain and spices. A fantasy land called Cathay grew in their imagination and evolved into the fashion for Chinoiserie which reached its height during the eighteenth century, mainly as decoration on wallpapers, porcelain, laquerwork and textiles. In 1600 the East India Company was formed, which had direct trading links with England and principally exchanged fabrics.

Since Elizabethan times castles had given way to manor houses, and the growing middle class built town and country houses that became increasingly more comfortable. The bed was of particular importance and status, and was hung with heavy curtains

Sea of Life: *design for a bolster cushion using a family of whales. Worked on a space-dyed furnishing fabric of linen/cotton twill using dyed crewel wools. Stitches include cretan, satin, stem, various fillings and crossed buttonhole edgings. Designed and worked by Jeanette* Durrant (PHOTOGRAPHY: GAVIN DURRANT)

and a valance, with covers and pillows completing the set. 'Bed furniture' was often worked by the lady of the house and her servants, who could call upon the services of a pattern drawer to design and outline the motifs for them. (Larger scale motifs were often worked entirely by professionals.) During the latter half of the seventeenth century it was fashionable for a mother to be sewing her crewelwork while her daughter worked on stumpwork, and many of the same symbols appear in both embroideries.

The essence of crewelwork is to use woollen threads to work a variety of stitches and fillings. If a simple structure and outline are established the embroidery can be worked directly onto the fabric in a spontaneous manner, adapting the motifs to fill any shape.

Crewelwork can form the basis of an exciting series of experiments using traditional stitches and fillings to create shapes and motifs. Use a limited palette of colour but with several shades for each, or space-dye threads and allow colour to occur in a random manner. Model the various shapes of a design by using open fillings to give light tones, and solid stitching to give darker ones. For more abstract work, isolate the basic elements of fillings, solid stitch, or edgings and allow them to mix and overlap. This method could be reversed, stitching the background and leaving the motifs void. The scale of the stitches could also be varied, or the stitches could be worked in white thread on a coloured background.

Crewelwork is not only decorative but makes a strong practical textile suitable for cushions, bags, shoes, waistcoats, or chair seats. A firm twill fabric such as linen/cotton union or a furnishing fabric gives good support to stitches and allows flowing shapes to be worked without too much distortion or puckering, although too large a scale twill can be difficult to stitch accurately. Silk or wool twill for finer work could be used, but would need a backing fabric and the stitching worked in silk threads. Fabric could be natural, dyed or printed.

Working in a frame keeps the fabric flat and the laidwork even. Modern crewel wool is a fine two-ply wool in a wide range of colours. White crewel wool, fine weaving or hand-spun wool could be dyed at home to your own colour scheme using fibre reactive

Whale World: *End of bolster cushion with whales worked in cretan, satin and stem stitch, and water and continents in French knots, bullion knots and crossed buttonhole edging. Designed and worked by Jeanette Durrant* (PHOTOGRAPHY: GAVIN DURRANT)

Man's World: *end of a bolster cushion with clouds worked in stem stitch and crossed buttonhole edging, and continents in satin stitch overlaid with grids and filling stitches. Designed and worked by Jeanette Durrant* (PHOTOGRAPHY: GAVIN DURRANT)

or acid dyes. Large-eyed crewel needles should be used. Work with a short length of thread, approximately 38.5–45.5cm (15–18in), and keep moving the eye of the needle and twisting the thread during stitching.

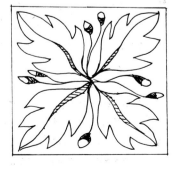

Different basic structures to support designs for cushions (DRAWING: JEANETTE DURRANT)

For inspiration, the local fauna or flora, wild flowers, herbs, vegetables, insects and animals could be used, or the herbals with their strong simple designs. With many exotic animals, birds and plants becoming extinct, old favourites like the Macaw parrot, cowslips or the swallowtail butterfly could soon become as remote to modern man as the imaginary world of Cathay or the 'beastes' of the herbals. Unexplored depths of the sea or universe give ample scope for the imagination to range freely, and crewelwork is still an ideal way to record them.

A family of whales is the design source for a bolster cushion, chosen because their flowing lines lend themselves well to the continuous rounded shape; and the ends of the cushion feature seas and continents. The embroidery is worked on a space-dyed furnishing fabric of linen/cotton twill using dyed crewel wools. Stitches include cretan, satin, stem, various fillings and crossed buttonhole edgings, with highlights worked in linen threads withdrawn from the background fabric.

The working of this cushion led to ideas for future work, using other wildlife and local fauna as the design source, to create a series of cushions and ultimately garments and accessories.

CHAPTER FIVE

RAISED EMBROIDERY ON COIFS

Muriel Best

THE RAISED embroidery of the seventeenth century developed from its beginnings in the samplers of the early 1600s to the elaborate panels, caskets and mirror frames of the latter half of the century. The coiling stems, flowers, leaves and motifs of insects, snails, birds and animals which were characteristic features of the Elizabethan era, prevailed well into the seventeenth century. The embroidery has a charm and fascination in design, colour and stitching which can still be appreciated today, as fortunately there are many fine examples preserved in museums and private collections.

In general, the linen cap or coif was shaped to form a hood when worn; the sides were curved, and were occasionally trimmed with gold lace, and the straight side had tying strings attached. The woman's coif which is illustrated here is a typical example of its type and period, dating from the early seventeenth century. The scrolling design reflects the patterns which were being used in sculpture and in wood-carving at that time, and the flowers are a reminder of the growing interest in gardens, which culminated in the splendid Italianate style when grottos, fountains and decorative pools were included towards the end of the century.

The repeating pattern of coiling stems continues all over, regardless of the outer shape of the coif. Flowers such as the pansy, rose, columbine, cornflower, the pods of the borage and pea, grapes and leaves are enclosed in the coiling stems, and the whole is interspersed with caterpillars and butterflies. There are shades of blue, green, pink, red and yellow silks on a linen background with some use of silver-gilt thread, silver strip and spangles. In spite of the age of the coif it remains bright and fresh in appearance with very little evidence of wear.

The stitches are varied and in some cases quite complicated. The coiling stems are in plaited braid stitch using silver-gilt thread; some flowers are worked in trellis stitch and others in different forms of detached buttonhole. The top half of the peascods are detached and stand away from the background to reveal tiny silver peas within. The outer edge of the coif is trimmed with chain stitch in silver-gilt thread.

It is the minute detail in this embroidery which is well worth studying, and the use of the composite stitches is particularly interesting; for instance, although detached buttonhole in its various forms is quite frequently used in contemporary work, trellis stitch as it is worked here is seldom seen. Plaited braid stitch too, is not popular, probably because it is complicated and time-consuming to work out. It is difficult to say categorically whether a coif such as this one would have been worked by a professional or within the home under the supervision of the lady of the house, or indeed by the lady herself. Certainly there were many fine amateur needlewomen, and if one had the money to buy the materials, what better way to spend one's leisure than embroidering items to beautify oneself and the home.

The counterpart of the woman's coif was the man's nightcap, though it was not in fact to be worn in bed but for indoor and informal wear. It was shaped to fit the head in the form of half an egg, sometimes with a turned-up brim. In some portraits of the period elderly men can occasionally be seen wearing their nightcaps; however, coifs are rarely in evidence in the portraits of women, who obviously preferred to be dressed in their best for public viewing.

The coif illustrated measures 25.5 x 43cm (10 x 17in) and was given by Lady Mary Cayley.

Antique embroidery is now highly prized and many of us have modest collections of textiles.

(above) *Woman's coif, English: the design of coiling stems encloses motifs of flowers and insects. The background is of linen and the embroidery is worked in coloured silks, silver-gilt thread and silver strip. The stitches include varieties of buttonhole, trellis, plaited braid and heavy chain*
EG no 161; *early seventeenth century; 25.5 x 43cm (10 x 17in); given by Lady Mary Cayley*
(PHOTOGRAPHY: DUDLEY MOSS)

(left) *Detail of the embroidery*
(PHOTOGRAPHY: DUDLEY MOSS)

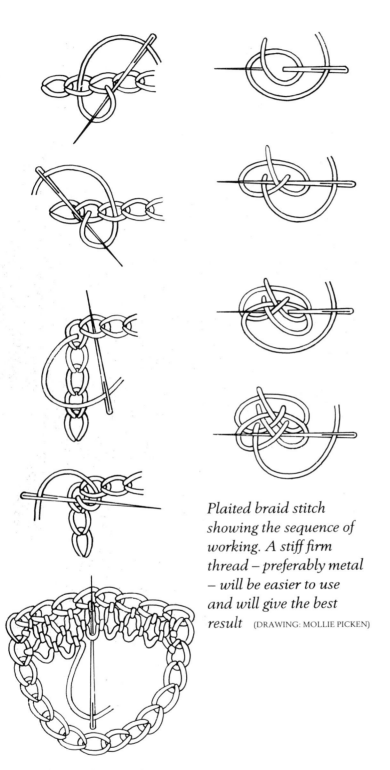

Plaited braid stitch showing the sequence of working. A stiff firm thread – preferably metal – will be easier to use and will give the best result (DRAWING: MOLLIE PICKEN)

Trellis stitch is worked on a foundation of chain stitches using a buttonhole stitch, working to and fro up into the loops of the previous row. This gives

a diagonal weave. The stitches do not enter the fabric, as in detached buttonhole stitch (DRAWING: MOLLIE PICKEN)

Modern methods of conservation mean that many fine examples (though probably priced beyond the reach of most of us) are displayed in museums and stately homes for us to study and enjoy.

It is interesting to note that while we are constantly trying out new materials and experimenting with various techniques we nevertheless keep looking over our shoulders to the past, and our interest in the new is equalled by our fascination with what has gone before. It is not difficult to find similarities in our work to that of our embroidery predecessors.

Stitches comprise just one of the avenues of study open to us. Many of the stitches used in the past are still in frequent use today while other more complicated ones are rarely worked. For example when choosing stitches for a piece of work, plaited braid stitch is unlikely to feature very high on the list, in fact it is probably not even considered. It looks difficult and complicated to do, and indeed it is quite hard to master. However, as the stitch was used extensively in the sixteenth and seventeenth centuries the embroiderers must have had an easier way of working it.

Perhaps one solution is to approach it via plain braid stitch; having learnt that, it is merely another step to conquer plaited braid. With this stitch it is important to choose an appropriate thread, one which is firm and will hold its shape, bearing in mind that seventeenth-century embroiderers are usually shown to have worked it in a metal thread. One way of mastering the stitch would be to try it out on a large scale using a loosely woven fabric as a background and a thick thread; subsequently a thinner thread and a smaller scale would be easier to handle.

Another stitch which features in the raised embroidery of the seventeenth century is trellis, which is similar to the family of buttonhole stitches and in particular detached buttonhole. It is a versatile stitch which can be used either to cover quite highly padded motifs or to create a flat covering. The traditional method of working is to start by outlining the shape with chain stitch; this acts as a basis for the attached knotted loops. However, this is not really necessary as a row of back stitches is quite adequate as a foundation and allows more flexibility for working. A smooth thread is preferable, as any thread with a pronounced twist will give an uneven finish. Using a round-ended tapestry needle will make it easier to work this knotted loop stitch. Once again, the more proficient one becomes, the finer the thread that can be used.

These stitches are attractive and it seems a pity to allow them to be forgotten; maybe now is the time to revive them, along with other more complex stitches from the past. Nowadays the embroiderers' stitch vocabulary appears to be limited to a relatively simple range, quick and easy to do with the accent on creating texture and the play of light by using directional straight stitches.

With such a rich heritage of stitches it seems almost shameful to neglect the great variety at our disposal; it may take a little detective work to discover how some of them are worked, but that can be a fascinating area of study in itself. A good discipline might be to learn a new stitch to use with each new project, exploring the possibilities of various thicknesses of threads and scale of working.

The encrusted surfaces of many of the seventeenth-century embroideries, made richer by the use of coloured silks, metal threads and tiny spangles, have a timeless appeal, providing inspiration for contemporary embroiderers.

In the modern piece illustrated here it is the raised effect of some of the stitches which has been taken as a starting-point. Cord, braid and string have been used as a foundation over which a variety of stitches have been worked; these include Van Dyke, buttonhole, fly and cretan stitch. Further stitches worked on a flat surface include heavy chain, braid, plaited braid and trellis; tiny spangles dot the background.

The ribbed design of flowing lines echoes the coiling stems used to contain the motifs in the coif. Such a piece could be made into a small decorative purse based on a simple rectangular shape similar to those given as presents during the seventeenth century.

Extra embellishments in the form of tassels and cords would be appropriate. There are many possibilities to be explored in this rich and tactile form of embroidery.

A line drawing of a seventeenth-century purse and a pincushion (DRAWING: MURIEL BEST)

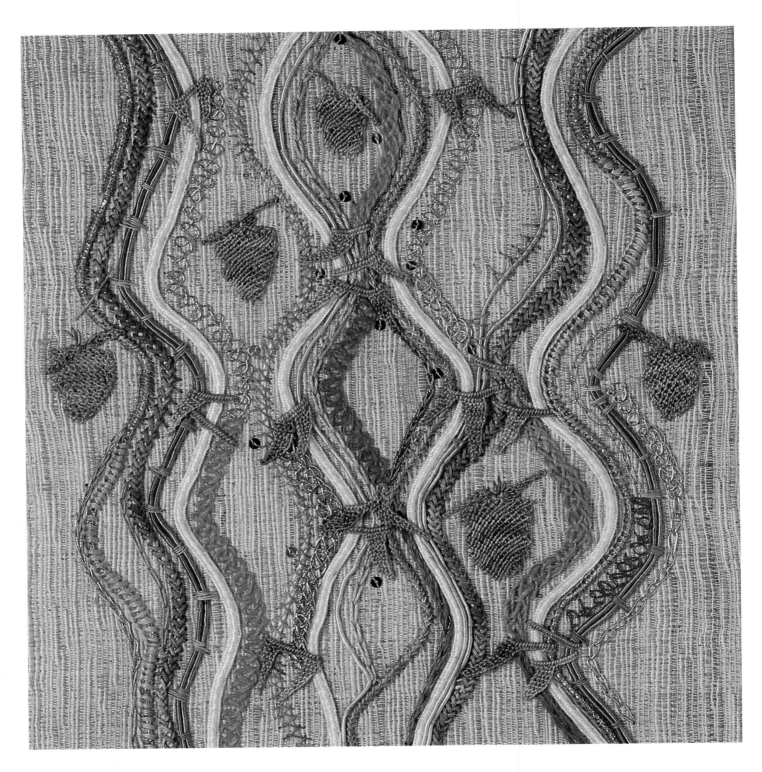

A design of curving lines, some of which are raised by stitching over cords and string. The background is a textured silk, and the embroidery is worked in spaced-dyed silks of various thicknesses and in metal threads. The stitches used include some of those found in the seventeenth-century coif. Designed and worked by Muriel Best (PHOTOGRAPHY: JIM PASCOE)

(right) *Coloured pencil drawing showing how the embroidery could be used for a purse*
(DRAWING: MURIEL BEST)

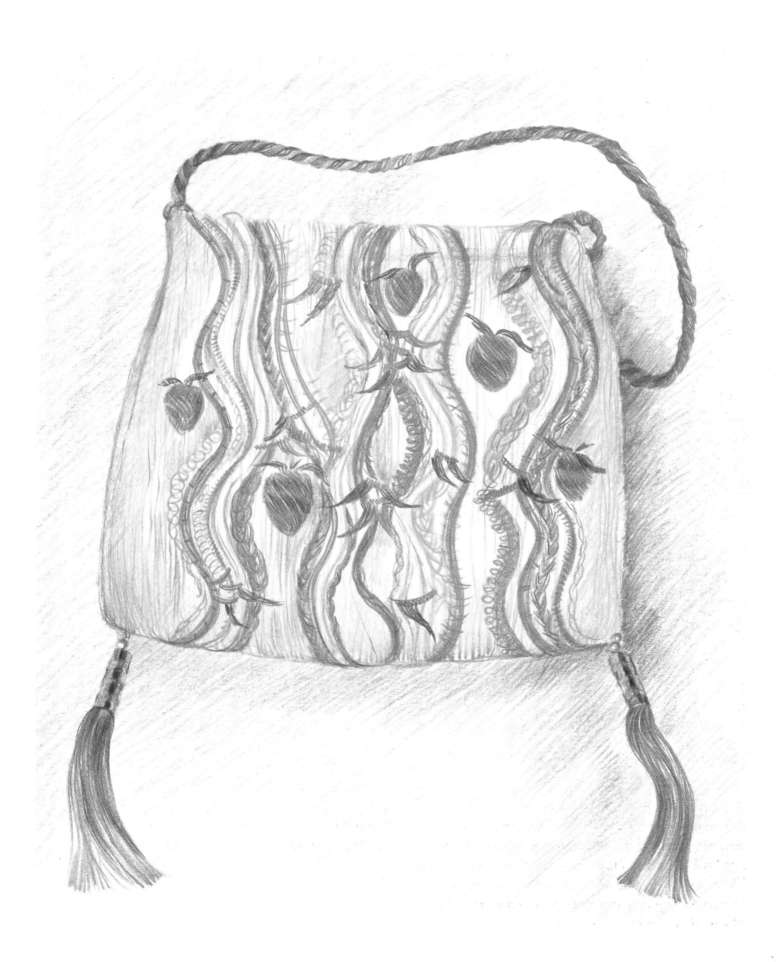

CHAPTER SIX

DECORATIVE MOTIFS

Valerie Campbell-Harding

THIS FLOWER motif chosen from the Guild Collection is a late sixteenth- or early seventeenth-century fragment depicting a pink (then also called a gillyflower), which was a symbol of love. This flower is likely to have been used within a trellis linking the motifs in a diaper pattern, a frequent design device of the period. The embroidery is worked in black silk counted-thread patterns on linen with 96 threads per inch/2.5cm. This would have been impossible to count accurately so some of the stitches have pierced the threads of the linen giving a slightly uneven effect which is delightful. It is edged in chain stitch worked in silver-gilt thread, with 20 stitches per inch/2.5cm. The flower measures 7cm (2¾in) wide and 8cm (3¼in) deep.

Another frequently seen pattern of the period is of scrolling stems connecting applied slips of flowers, with stem and foliage, similar in style to this one. A slip is an embroidered motif which was worked separately and applied to another fabric, building up a design. Single slips, often worked in tent stitch, were applied as powdered (or spot) motifs together with figures and insects.

The habit of working separate motifs was extremely common and was (and is) also much used in regalia, ecclesiastical embroidery in Europe, and also silk embroidery in other countries such as China. One reason for this is the ease of working on small pieces and later applying them to larger fabrics. Another reason is that it is difficult to embroider on a fabric such as velvet, so the embroidery was worked on linen and applied to velvet when finished.

What is particularly appealing is the fineness of the embroidery and the delightful fragments of pattern – fragmented because of wear, the combination of geometric patterns and the organic shape of the flower, and the whole idea of working separate slips of embroidery to apply to another piece of embroidery or to each other.

When using a source such as this for designing a contemporary embroidery, it is important to consider all the aspects of the original and then decide which of them to use. It would be possible to use the slip idea, the shape of the flower, the colour scheme, the blackwork patterns and the tiny scale, all as elements in a new piece of embroidery. However, the chances are that it would end up looking like the original. A dramatic change in colour or scale would avoid this, and so would a change of stitch method. As the scale is enchanting, it was decided to keep the embroidery small, but to change the colour scheme and use machine embroidery instead of hand to help break away from simply copying the original. The blackwork patterns could be enlarged and made into printing blocks cut from a potato or a rubber (depending on the size of the end result) and printed on fabrics. These little patterns also worked well as repeat patterns drawn on a computer, both as regular patterns or more informal ones, with overlapping shapes. They could be adapted to automatic patterns on a computerised sewing machine and used to build up a rich surface. On a larger scale, the shapes within the patterns could be presented as separate pieces of applied fabric with added stitchery, thus building up a background for the slips.

A drawing of the pink was scanned into the computer and the size reduced. It was pasted on top of some of the enlarged geometric patterns to see the effect, and then duplicated to make all-over designs. Some ideas for the complete design were also drawn on the computer, which produces alternatives so quickly that many ideas can be explored in a short space of time. The black and white computer print-

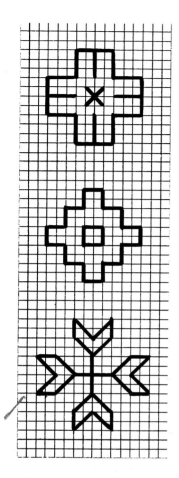

Single pink motif within a trellis

(below) *The motif has been scanned into the computer and repeated to make an all-over pattern*

(above) *Some of the blackwork motifs from the sample drawn on graph paper*
(DRAWING: MOLLIE PICKEN)

(right) *An Elizabethan slip in blackwork, edged with silver-gilt chain stitch*
EG no 206; 7 x 8.25cm (2³/4 x 3¹/4in)
(PHOTOGRAPHY: DUDLEY MOSS)

(below right) *Detail of finished embroidery. Designed and worked by Valerie Campbell-Harding*
(PHOTOGRAPHY: PETER READ)

(opposite) *The finished bag (23 x 43cm [9 x 17in] including the tassels) displayed on its own board showing the designs, samples and experiments. Machine embroidery, including straight, zig-zag, couching and automatic patterns, and granite and looping stitch, was worked on screen-printed fabric, appliqué and woven ribbons. Designed and worked by Valerie Campbell-Harding*
(PHOTOGRAPHY: PETER READ)

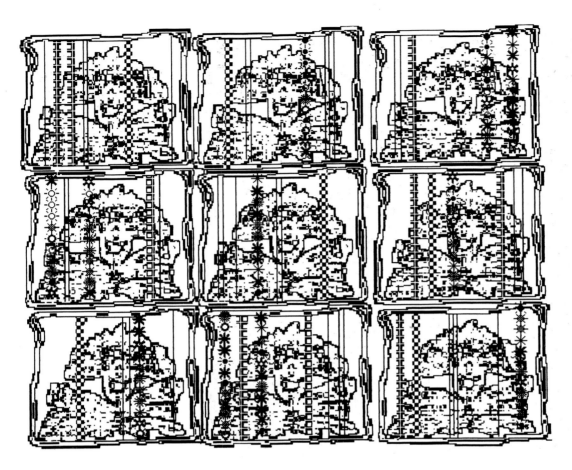

The scanned pink placed over the blackwork pattern

outs were coloured using ink and bleach with added streaks of coloured and metallic paint, and drawn into with a gold pen.

Initial thoughts were to use the computer to design the background embroidery using larger shapes taken from the blackwork patterns and applying separate flowers within the larger empty areas of the pattern, or on top of a single pattern. Then the idea of working double slips occurred – small squares of rich embroidery including automatic machine patterns, with separately embroidered flowers applied onto them. The squares would be joined to each other, or applied to a background, to make a bag. Then a large board would be made to hang on the wall which would display the finished bag and also the designs and experiments that appeared while planning the final result.

It is not always a good idea to decide beforehand what the finished piece is to be, as further ideas often appear while working through the design process. However in this case, the bag-board was destined to be part of a half-finished series of a Wall of Bags, with

bag-boards, panels, and separate bags, all making a richly textured, undulating surface which could be altered and changed.

The problem of designing from a traditional embroidery was quite difficult, as the tendency was either to copy the original, or at least some aspects of it; or to move so far away that source material might as well not have been used at all. It seemed important to keep the shape of the flower and the geometry of the blackwork fillings. In order to add extra elements, the whole range of Elizabethan costume and embroidery was looked at and the colour scheme of black, gold, bronze and cream, with small flecks of red, copper and blue-green, was taken from the period. Richness of stitchery as well as of colour was another important element of the period, easily achieved now on the sewing machine.

Having worked through some design ideas, the next stage was to paint some fabric to stitch onto. Silhouettes of the flower were cut out of paper and used as a resist during screen printing on various fabrics, with coloured paints and gold and copper

This idea of a simple repeat pattern was discarded in favour of a more informal design using mixed rectangles, pinks and borders

metal powders. Gold leaf was applied to some of these printed flowers using PVA and gin, a process worked out with a gilding friend. Rectangles of fabric were then cut out, each with a printed flower in the centre; they were backed with felt and machine stitched all over with straight lines in variegated metallic threads and a few bands of automatic patterns in black thread. The edges of the pieces were then burnt in a candle flame to avoid the raw look of a cut edge. One area of the bag uses a piece made of woven and stitched tubular ribbons, painted after stitching.

The rich texture on the wide band at the base of the bag, and for the whole of the back of the bag, was built up using a screen printed base with strips of transparent metallic fabrics and lengths of cords, ribbons and braids, all stitched down with automatic patterns that resemble blackwork patterns. This avoided the problem of using them as fillings which would have been too much like the original. Rows of machine loops (using the looping foot) were added between the couching to give even more texture to

contrast with the flat machining, and to raise the edges of the fabric strips.

Finally, three separate flowers were worked as slips on fabric shapes applied to black muslin using granite stitch (repeating tiny circles worked so solidly that no fabric finally shows) in variegated metallic threads, each one a different colour. The flowers were cut out and the edges burnt to neaten them and give a darker line to show up against the background.

The separate rectangles and borders of embroidery were first laid on a backing of black felt bonded with transparent gold fabric and stitched to it. Strips of solid stitching over applique made other borders, with added squares of felt-backed fabric applied to emphasise the geometric shapes that were within the blackwork patterns. The flower slips were laid on three of the rectangles and stitched down securely with more granite stitch. Finally, machine-stitched cords were made, some couched down over one of the gold-leaf flowers, and others used to attach the tassels to the bottom border.

CHAPTER SEVEN

STITCHING WITH SILK AND RIBBONS

Muriel Best

IN THE LATTER part of the nineteenth century there was an increasing interest in what was termed 'fancy needlework'. The revival of embroidery as a creative craft was perhaps a reaction to the introduction of the sewing machine, which had been developed from the first half of the century until in the 1860s it reached the stage of replacing handworkers for professional dress and furnishing decoration.

The Royal School of Needlework was founded in 1872 with the intention of restoring decorative hand needlework and giving employment to poor gentlewomen. Similar bodies, such as the Ladies' Work Society and the Decorative Needlework Society were also formed at this time. All this interest in handwork permeated through to the amateur needlewoman, who was able to buy transfers, fabrics, braids, beads, ribbons and threads in great variety. Magazines were published with instructions for decorating household linen and underwear; patterns were given for crocheted and knitted items as well as embroidery techniques and stitches. Sachets were made for holding a number of diverse objects, handkerchiefs and nightwear being among the most popular.

These magazines catering for 'fancy needlework' were to continue into the 1900s with such titles as *Fancy Needlework Illustrated*, and *The Home Book of Fancy Stitchery* edited by Flora Klickman. Also edited by Flora was the invaluable *Mistress of the Little House* which detailed the proper management of the small house including advice on . . . *Providing the Houselinen, Training the Young Servant and Cleaning the Stairs*.

The night dressing-case illustrated here is late nineteenth century and is typical of its period, presenting a professional appearance which suggests that it might well have been purchased partly worked, finished by the home embroiderer, and then made up in a commercial workroom. The case is of cream silk, with a lining of fine pink silk, and thin wadding (batting) sandwiched between them to give extra body. The edges are trimmed with braid and a looped silk fringe and piping cord is sewn around the underside of the case to keep it firm.

The design on the front flap reflects the prevailing taste for garlands of flowers and elaborate bows. A formal fretwork border of couched narrow velvet ribbon contains the garlands of flowers. The garlands, and a repeating pattern of circlets, are worked in a twisted silk thread in satin and stem stitch, with some of the flowers embroidered with a narrow silk ribbon. This ribbon was specially woven for use in embroidery, and was shaded in tints of one colour. Used like an ordinary thread in a large-eyed crewel needle, it was pulled through the background, and worked best on a closely woven linen or silk sufficiently strong enough to bear the strain of pulling the ribbon through. A 'malore' of steel or ivory was sometimes used for holding down the ribbon to prevent it from twisting. Lengths of 31 to 46cm (12 to 18in) were best, so that the ribbon was not worn by too much pulling through, and a knot was made to hold it in place when starting, and again to finish off.

The roses are worked in detached chain or lazy-daisy stitch in narrow shaded pink ribbon, and the tiny forget-me-knots are worked in small straight

Night dressing-case. British, late nineteenth century.
An envelope-shaped case of cream silk edged with silk
fringe and braid. The formal fretwork border of narrow
velvet ribbon contains garlands of flowers worked in
shaded silk ribbons and silk threads
EG no 3795; 45 x 57cm (17 1/2 x 22 1/2in)
(PHOTOGRAPHY: DUDLEY MOSS)

stitches in blue, with yellow silk French knots for their centres. Stem stitch is used for some of the leaves, with rows of stem stitch making additional ribbon-like swags around the garlands. A fine silk chenille thread is couched to make a long repeating border pattern of small circles, further decorated with long-tailed French knots. This form of embroidery was very popular in the last quarter of the nineteenth century when it was known as 'Rococo work'. An interesting glimpse into the era is provided by copies of old periodicals – *La Mode Illustre 1867 (Journal de la Famille)*, for instance, makes fascinating reading. Ribbons are ruched and folded into complicated patterns to ornament dresses, with the folds often held in place with tiny beads.

Fashions and life-styles change, and the customs and practices of the late Victorian era may seem somewhat inappropriate today; for instance the

night dressing-case is a symbol of a more leisurely age, like handkerchief sachets and pochettes. However, the practice of making containers to hold objects continues, be they bags, purses, boxes or packets. It is the making of precious packets to hold special objects which is explored here. Many large department stores offer a gift-wrapping service, but how much more satisfying to make one's own wrapping or packet, suiting the style to the contents and the recipient. The Japanese have elevated the practice

Illustration showing a variety of papers, both decorated and handmade, and a paper packet
(PHOTOGRAPHY: JIM PASCOE)

tice of wrapping objects to an art form, and nothing is considered too humble for their attention.

A variety of materials from silk to paper can be used for making packages, and the nature of the contents will influence the choice. Moreover, if the right colour or effect is not available commercially there are so many paints and dyes on the market, and so many ways of using them, that obtaining a desired effect is always within reach. For instance fabrics can be random-dyed, spray-dyed or stencilled, and papers too can be decorated in various ways – using a wax resist, bleaching out colour, texturing with paste and paint, and marbling. The fibrous papers

from the East, especially Japan and Thailand, are attractive to use and come in a range of weights and textures, ranging from thin tissue-like papers to heavier ones embedded with leaves and straws.

Making paper is an exciting process, and from your first somewhat thick and lumpy pieces you will soon find it easier to control the thickness of the pulp and produce quite fine results. The accidental irregularities are part of the charm of handmade paper: if perfect paper were required every time then it might as well be a commercial product.

Although it is possible to make complicated packets involving intricate folding, it is often the simplest designs which are the most effective. Those which rely on the materials used for their effect provide opportunities for further embellishment in the form of fastenings using braids and decorative

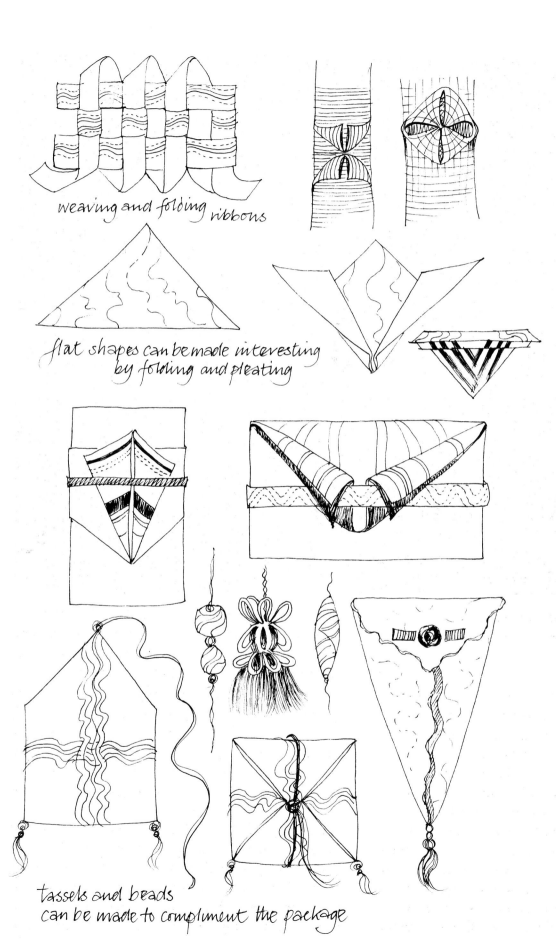

Line drawings of further ideas for packages and their decorations
(DRAWING: MURIEL BEST)

weaving and folding ribbons

flat shapes can be made interesting by folding and pleating

tassels and beads can be made to compliment the package

An example of decorated paper, produced by monoprinting

tassels. Plaited ribbons and silks, together with interesting beads of various sizes, become part of the whole project. Narrow silk ribbons are available, and if you are very lucky, some of the original Victorian shaded ribbon may be found, hidden away in an antique shop.

The packages in the illustration are designed to be displayed together rather than used for utilitarian purposes. Both fabrics and papers are used in their construction, with ribbon used for stitching as well as for decorative ties. Obviously too much stitching through paper will weaken the surface, so the stitches are kept quite simple. Interlacing stitch is an

effective method of joining two sides together and is a decorative feature in itself, as are the beads, which are made of modelling clay and specifically designed to coordinate the whole package.

The packages are all rectangular like the night dressing-case, but they differ from each other in the materials that are used, and in the decoration and the details of fastening. In one package the corners of the flap are turned back to show the different coloured

lining, and in another a circle of *papier mâché* beads is used as a fastening which becomes the decorative feature.

Many variations can be made on one theme, and it would be an interesting exercise to take one shape and see how you could alter its appearance by different means. For instance the crisp folds of paper would look quite different from the softer edges of folded fabric, and bright contrasting colours would

Three packages based on the envelope shape of the night dressing-case. Paper and silk are used in the construction, and extra decoration is added in the form of stitching, cords and tassels. Designed and worked by Muriel Best (PHOTOGRAPHY: JIM PASCOE)

be different from the muted subtle tones of one colour. A whole body of work might be built around this idea.

CHAPTER EIGHT

LACE AND LAYERS

Sylvia Bramley

THE EMBROIDERY illustrated is a fan mount, made around 1900 using the technique called 'Carrickmacross lace'. It was never made into a fan and therefore shows no sign of wear.

The Art Nouveau design, using plant forms with exaggerated curves, is typical of the period. It is created from pansies and butterflies and in the centre of the mount the stems twist around each other with great sensitivity. The design of the applied cambric is cleverly worked so that the outside edge of the applied cotton is unbroken. The edge is finished with 'twirling', made of couched loops, which gives a distinctive finish to Carrickmacross lace.

The fan mount is cream throughout, and beautifully made, using fine machine-made square net, part of which is embroidered with filling stitches; many of these can be found in *The Complete Encyclopedia of Needlework* by Thérèse de Dillmont. Fine cotton is used for the appliqué and the design is outlined with a cream lace thread, which is couched with fine thread, probably a no 50, which would be used for the filling stitches as well.

Unlike many other embroidery techniques which have ancient origins, Carrickmacross lace is relatively recent; it is also well documented, particularly in Nellie O'Cleirigh's book *Carrickmacross Lace*. It is an Irish lace, and is a combination of appliqué and embroidered net which was developed during the early part of the nineteenth century by Mrs Grey Porter who lived near Carrickmacross in County Monaghan. Mrs Grey Porter had seen examples of appliqué lace in Italy in 1816 and was sufficiently interested to learn how to make it herself. She then taught the technique to her maid Ann Steadman, and together they started a school, which became popular for young women anxious to learn a skill, and subsequently a living. Machine-made net

had recently been developed and this provided a base for the appliqué. The fortunate timing of this invention by the Heathcote Co must have been a major factor in the development of Carrickmacross lace, since handmade net would have been far too time-consuming and expensive.

The social need to provide work for girls gave impetus to the formation of more schools, and in time a girl's earnings undoubtedly made a significant contribution to the family income. Indeed, in the 1840s during the famine years in Ireland following the potato crop failure, the income from lace-making must have been a lifeline for some families.

The net – the basis of Carrickmacross lace – was originally a square mesh, although nowadays it is more likely to be hexagonal. A fine cotton or organdie is used for the applied shapes. These two fabrics should be the same colour, ideally either cream or white, and the two fabrics are initially treated as one with the surplus cotton cut away after the outlining has been worked. A thick lace thread or crochet cotton is used to outline the design, couched down with a fine thread which is also used for any filling stitches. It is important that the thread should have a good twist and not in any way be fluffy. A very fine needle is used throughout. Lace-makers' scissors are an advantage as they have a small knob on one side to prevent the net being cut.

The complete design including the loops is transferred onto good quality tracing paper, using Indian ink to make a strong black line which will show through both net and cotton. It is useful to place a sheet of white cartridge paper underneath the tracing paper to make the traced line easier to see.

The net is placed over the tracing and cartridge paper, and the design is tacked through the three layers, starting at the centre and working to the

(above) *The centre of the wedding veil showing the main motif. Designed and worked by Sylvia Bramley*
(PHOTOGRAPHY: SYLVIA BRAMLEY)

(left) *The complete veil, hanging in folds as it would appear in use. Worked in machine-embroidery threads including a white pearlised metallic thread. A swing needle was used for the pulled work section, and the edges of the veil were finished with a shell edging. Designed and worked by Sylvia Bramley*
(PHOTOGRAPHY: SYLVIA BRAMLEY)

edges. Then the net is covered with the cotton fabric and the process is repeated. It is important, at this stage, that the design still shows through all the layers, which is why a strong black line is necessary on the tracing paper.

The thicker thread is held over the design line and, working from right to left, is couched down with the thinner thread, stitching through the cotton and the net, but remembering not to stitch through the tracing paper. It should be kept as one continu-

An embroidered fan mount, made around 1900, in Carrickmacross lace. The materials include a fine machine-made square net, part of which is embroidered with filling stitches
EG(L) no 1049; 16 x 46.5cm (6¼ x 18¼in)
(PHOTOGRAPHY: DUDLEY MOSS)

ous line throughout the embroidery and the stitches should be kept fairly close together.

A decorative edge is made by forming the thicker thread into loops, each one held in place with two small stitches placed inside the loop. The loops should be the same size throughout. When the

stitching is finished, the tacking threads and tracing paper are removed and the surplus cotton is cut away to the edge of the stitched design, taking great care not to cut the net. The net may now be embroidered with needlemade filling stitches.

When considering this piece as a source of inspira-tion for a contemporary embroidery, it was decided to retain the delicacy of the Carrickmacross lace; and as such lace was often used for wedding veils, a short veil of machine-embroidered silk muslin seemed ap-propriate.

In the course of researching the fan mount, col-

The design taken from part of the fan mount
(DRAWING: SYLVIA BRAMLEY)

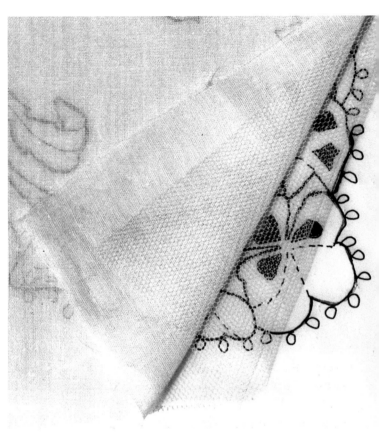

Twirling; the drawing shows the position of the stitches holding down the loops used to edge the lace. The loops can be spaced or touching   (DRAWING: MOLLIE PICKEN)

The layers used, ie the drawing covered by the net covered by the cambric   (PHOTOGRAPHY: SYLVIA BRAMLEY)

The layers are firmly tacked together to prevent any movement during the stitching; the outline couching and twirling is started   (PHOTOGRAPHY: SYLVIA BRAMLEY)

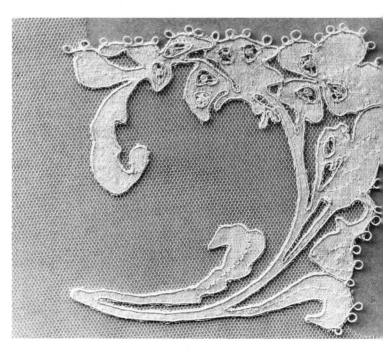

The finished sample showing the excess cambric cut away   (PHOTOGRAPHY: SYLVIA BRAMLEY)

our slides were taken to be used for future reference, and in order to make a working drawing of the fan, a slide was projected (actual size) onto a sheet of cartridge paper. During this drawing process the great sensitivity of the design became even more apparent, and I was particularly attracted to the motif with sinuous twisted stems. So, this motif was chosen for further development.

Still using the projector, the motif was enlarged to different sizes, and the paper was moved so that one layer of the design could be drawn over a previous drawing. Using a slide and a projector in this way soon leads to innumerable other shapes and patterns, both abstract and realistic.

The centre of the veil is a formal pattern, made from the chosen motif being repeated into a circle. A layer of silk organza was applied to part of the design using a sewing machine with a wing needle, which is sometimes called a hemstitch needle. (This process tends to stiffen the fabric, so it was used sparingly, as a veil needs to be fluid.) The corners were worked using the same motif but on a different scale and

differently placed. For this part of the veil a twin needle was used with a white pearlised metallic thread on the bobbin and a very fine polyester thread in the needle. The wing needle was used for the pulled work section, and the edges of the veil were finished with a shell edging.

Whilst working the sample of Carrickmacross lace it became obvious that the couched thread needed to be one continuous line, and that constant cutting or joining would spoil the work. This is similar to machine embroidery, where a continuous line is also wanted.

Other possibilities which suggested themselves during the initial stages were couched cord outlines to raise the surface, a variety of needlemade fillings, needle loops, and appliqué and cutwork. Numerous ideas for design based on the sinuous plant forms of the Art Nouveau period could be adapted to this form of embroidery. Although nowadays it is a neglected technique, there are many interesting possibilities for experiment using modern fabrics and threads.

Line drawings worked from a projected slide
(DRAWING: SYLVIA BRAMLEY).

CHAPTER NINE

WESSEX STITCHERY

Constance Howard

THE TWO PURSES illustrated are examples of Wessex stitchery, which was the brainchild of a Mrs Margaret M. Foster (who lived in Bath – hence 'Wessex'). She was a prolific embroiderer and her work spans the last part of the nineteenth century to the 1930s. There was an exhibition of her work in London in 1934 showing over three hundred pieces, including framed samplers and small objects.

These small purses are typical examples of Wessex work; the larger of the two is obviously designed for practical use as a holder for sewing and crochet accessories, and has a tiny pocket in one corner worked in a detached buttonhole or Ceylon stitch. The small square-shaped purse has a lettered panel included in the design, which says 'Here's dust of scented cedar trees to keep the moth away'. At first the embroidery appears very simple but on closer examination one can see that intricate patterns and rich decoration have been made from simple stitches. The embroidery is worked on the warp and weft of the fabric, but without counting the threads.

The chief feature of Wessex stitchery lies in the use of a limited number of stitches combined in a great variety of patterns to give a surprisingly decorative effect. The use of different thicknesses of thread

(right) *A detail of the stitching of one of the purses, showing lettering*

(PHOTOGRAPHY: DUDLEY MOSS)

(opposite) *Two small purses, examples of Wessex stitchery. The larger of the two is obviously designed for practical use as a holder for sewing and crochet accessories. The small square-shaped purse has a lettered panel included in the design* Smaller purse: EG no 22; 1983; 10 x 9cm (4 x 3 1/2in). Larger purse: EG no 24; 1983; 16 x 10cm (6 1/4 x 4in)

(PHOTOGRAPHY: DUDLEY MOSS)

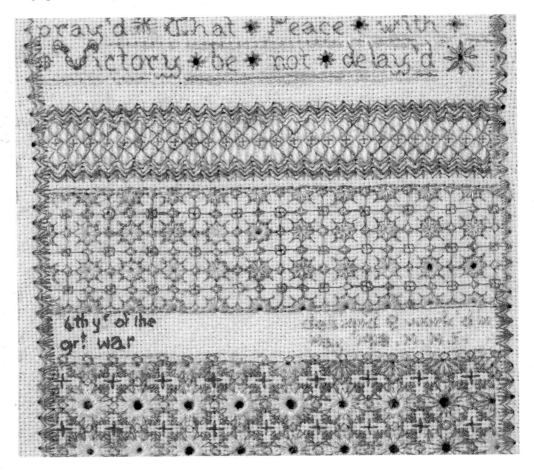

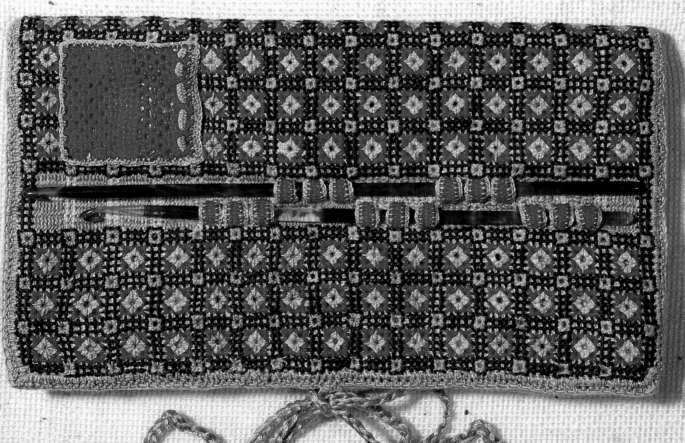

Here's dust of scented cedar trees to keep the moth away

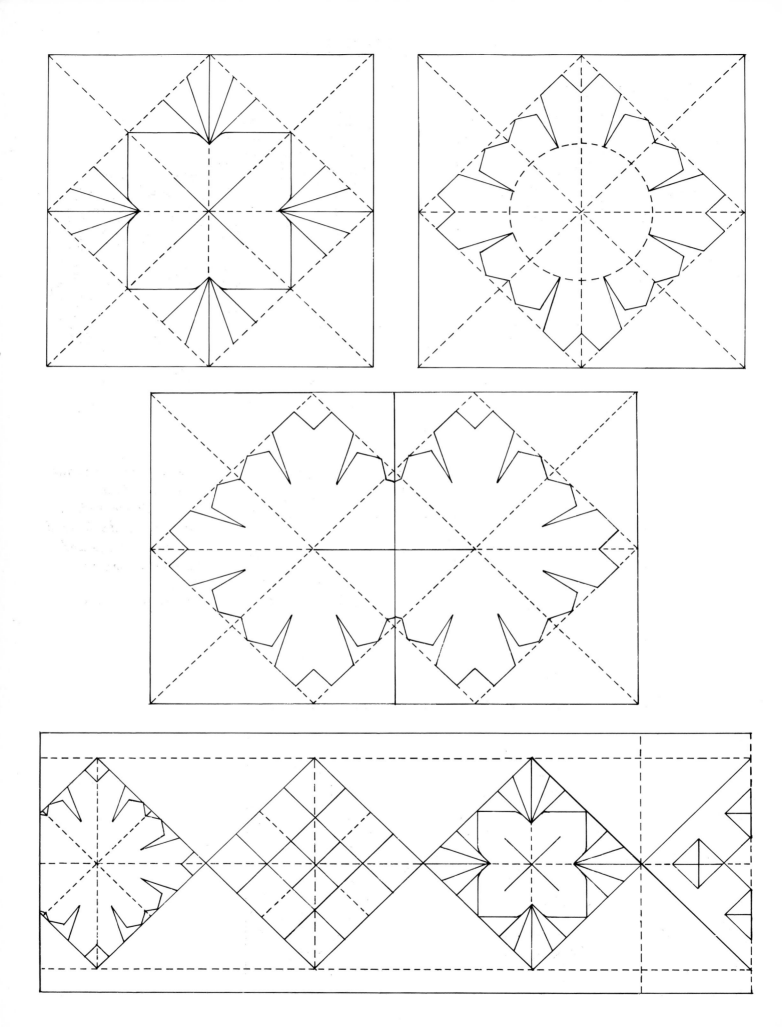

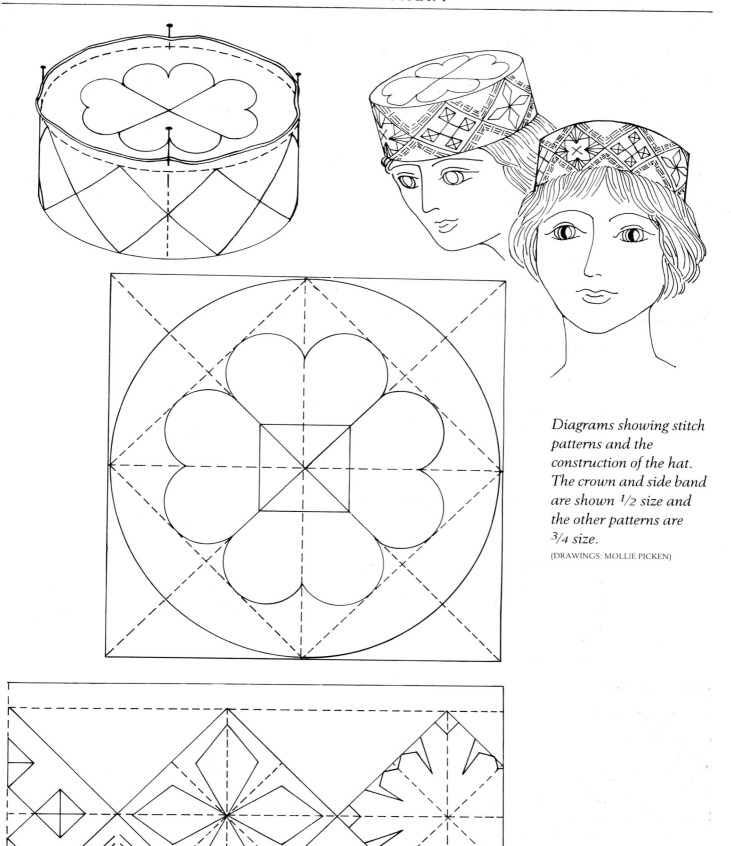

Diagrams showing stitch patterns and the construction of the hat. The crown and side band are shown 1/2 size and the other patterns are 3/4 size.

(DRAWINGS: MOLLIE PICKEN)

also suggests an affinity with filigree jewellery, where gold and silver wires mingle to make solid shapes – in contrast to finely fashioned, more open ones.

The embroidery was worked on hand-woven linen or cotton, in silk, linen or cotton threads, in monochrome, in one colour on a contrasting coloured background such as cream or red, or in several colours often on a natural linen ground. A blunt-eyed needle was advocated for the work, as threads of the fabric were often drawn together by the stitches to give an open-worked effect, or stitches were tied together. Long-tailed chain stitch was a special feature of the work, as by changing the lengths of the tail, the stitch could be manipulated to give an infinite number of patterns; these were sometimes combined with couching and weaving. Other stitches used were back, satin, chain, fly, straight and occasionally buttonhole. Mrs Foster often gave stitches special names, apart from their universal ones, to differentiate between certain patterns. These were called after persons or places and were sometimes explained in the lettering which is a strong feature of Wessex work.

No design on paper was involved: Mrs Foster said that the patterns would evolve themselves, and claimed that a good knowledge of stitches was all that was necessary. The overall effect of much of the work was often complicated, but it was obtained with simple stitches that in combination resulted in the jewel-like effect that is so attractive. As the stitchery was worked with the warp and weft of the fabric, the design was geometric and many patterns are built up on this basic structure. Some motifs were detached, others are closely worked repetitious patterns. Squares of stitches surrounded with smaller squares, with a line of stitches in between, were a feature of some of the work. The lettering worked on many of the examples was arranged in strips or bands of words; some describing the reasons for the names,

The deep pill-box hat is designed to be worn quite straight on the head. There is a different pattern in each square, taken from the embroideries of Mrs Foster. All the patterns are much enlarged, and worked on material cut on the bias, the procedure for cloth hats. Designed and worked by Constance Howard

while others were mottoes or sayings. These bands were usually interspersed with square patterns.

The decorative appeal of this form of stitchery seems suitable not just for purses but also for clothing. Because the embroidery is worked on the warp and weft of the fabric, when the pattern is placed on the diagonal and worked on the straight of the grain, the result is quite different. It is this aspect which influenced the decision to make a hat, and a pillbox shape seemed suitable because several patterns could be used on the side band and crown.

The hat is made of unevenly woven, coarse linen in a dark mustard colour, and is cut on the true bias. In Mrs Foster's embroideries similar patterns recur, in small units placed close together, and this repetition gives a rich textural effect. For the decoration of the hat these patterns have been considerably enlarged, something easily accomplished given the basic geometric structure. The final patterns on the hat are developed from preliminary research and combined with some from the sampler illustrated.

The main structure lines of the embroidery are basted onto the material and removed as the stitching progresses, working on the straight grain. Drawing is not involved except for a template for the petals on the crown of the hat. The embroidery is worked mainly in a back stitch, with eyelet holes in overcast stitch. Extra weight is given to the back stitch by working one stitch over another in places.

Pattern pieces for the hat consist of a deep side band and a circular crown, whose width is one third the length of the band. The measurements may be reduced or enlarged as required, with the side band and crown adjusted accordingly. Seam allowances are added to both the pattern pieces. A non-slip lining and interfacing are also cut out.

To make up the hat the centres are marked on the side band and the crown both vertically and horizontally, and the interlining is basted to the wrong sides of the pieces. The back seam of the band and interlining are stitched and attached to the crown by pinning the opposite sides and easing the whole into position. After basting, it is then machined or hand-stitched together. The hem of the hat is turned up and catch-stitched to the lining, and finally the lining is sewn in place.

CHAPTER TEN

A DESIGN OF ITS TIME
(1920s–1990s)

Ros Chilcot

THE PANEL illustrated is unmounted and is described as a firescreen, designed and worked in 1927 by Madeleine Clifton. It has been much admired over the years as a fine example of her work, but unfortunately very little information can be found about the embroiderer herself. During the 1920s and 1930s her work appeared in some auspicious exhibitions, and received particular attention in reviews and articles in *The Studio* and *The Embroideress* magazines. She is mentioned alongside such famous contemporaries as the embroiderers Rebecca Crompton, Jessie Newberry and Louisa Pesel, and the painter Duncan Grant. The last, together with Roger Fry and Vanessa Bell, founded the Omega Workshops and began a movement to encourage and develop individual and intuitive methods of working within painting, pottery, furniture and embroidery.

In an article for *The Embroideress*, Madeleine Clifton wrote that she was interested in the relationship between fabric and threads, and that she enjoyed the brilliance achieved by varying the direction of stitches whilst keeping to one colour or tones of one colour. The effects of using a shiny thread at different angles appealed to her, and she enjoyed using stitches in conjunction with fabric, especially in the technique of appliqué.

This panel is worked on a natural, fine evenweave linen, embroidered with coloured silks, mainly in pastel tints, with some use of dark red, dark green and black. Abstract shapes derived from flower heads, a vase, and what appear to be palm trees, are bordered with a scroll design and embroidered mainly in pattern darning and pulled work.

As its name suggests, pattern darning is built up from an arrangement of counted-thread stitch blocks on an evenweave material. The stitch-line is continuous, worked row by row, and the pattern is developed by varying the length of the stitch and the amount of ground material picked up by the needle. A short effect can be achieved by working two shades of one colour at right angles to one another. Pulled work is another counted-thread technique, worked by pulling together the warp and weft threads of evenweave material to produce an open-work pattern or lacy appearance. Traditionally the thread should be the same weight and colour as the ground fabric. Both these techniques work well but need practice to achieve a good result.

The style of this embroidery has great subtlety; at a distance the colour and texture balance the picture beautifully. Madeleine Clifton's work shows a strong personal style, while in essence it undoubtedly belongs to the period of the 1920s and 1930s.

As an item for study, this piece from the Embroiderers' Guild Collection proved to be an interesting challenge. Thinking about the design, I decided to go back to the possible source of Madeleine Clifton's inspiration, and making a list of questions seemed a reasonable way to begin. What exactly was it all about? What does the imagery depict? Is it a still-life, a view, a garden, or something to do with the coast? The palm-tree shapes could be trees on a sea-shore, or they might represent no more than interestingly shaped foliage. This supposition triggered off a feeling about the place, and I had a

Drawings to illustrate some different approaches at the design stage, using conté sticks, torn and patterned paper (DRAWINGS: ROS CHILCOT)

An unmounted panel, described in a 1927 article as a firescreen, designed and worked by Madeleine Clifton. It is worked on a natural, fine evenweave linen, embroidered with coloured silks, mainly in pastel tints, with some dark red, dark green and black. The embroidery is mainly pattern darning and pulled work EG no 5288; 58 x 60cm (23 x 23½in)

(PHOTOGRAPHY: DUDLEY MOSS)

persistent impression that it was associated with somewhere like Nice or Cannes. The Mediterranean coast, especially that of the south of France, was very popular in the 1920s.

With little or no documentation about the embroidered panel, assumptions could be made with a certain amount of freedom. It was necessary to do some drawing to concentrate the mind on the job in hand and to explore as many avenues as possible. A still-life arrangement was set up using a jardinière, a pot-plant, a check tablecloth and some fruit, and a series of drawings made from it using a soft 3B pencil. A simple sketchy line-drawing was as good a way as any to get a basic feel for the outline and shapes. Next a number of explorations were made, working either from the still-life or from the previous drawings.

In these developments, conté sticks were used, simplifying the shape of the unworked areas and the main features while deliberately working into the spaces between the shapes. The last method is useful to isolate the background when an embroidery technique such as pattern darning or pulled work is being contemplated for a project.

An exercise using torn, coloured and patterned papers gave a good indication of whether the idea would work as appliqué with fabric; it also simplified the design. At this stage fabric samplers were tried out, too. I worked on evenweave in the traditional manner but used a wash of watercolour to give more interest to the background fabric before stitching. I also changed the method drastically by layering coloured transparent fabrics and laying black organza over a strong red base-fabric, and then machining patterns into it, and this gave a dramatic switch to a new idea. Thus the still-life aspect was kept and so was the pattern darning, but in much broader terms.

Pattern darning on a closely woven painted fabric such as calico or silk. The stitches are judged by eye to make up the patterns (PHOTOGRAPHY: ROS CHILCOT)

Another shift of ideas caused me to abandon the intention of using anything as regular as evenweave. In the course of the project I wondered what would happen to pattern darning should an unevenly woven fabric be used. I found that drawing out some squares on to calico with felt-tip fabric-markers gave a little tone to the bland background, and the stitches

(above) *Pattern darning, using the sewing machine. The red dupion is overlaid with black silk organza and pieces of coloured sheers which help the tone and colour and give impression of depth. Designed and worked by Ros Chilcot* (PHOTOGRAPHY: ROS CHILCOT)

(opposite) *The interpretation of the still-life was worked on a medium to heavy silk twill using silk dyes and gutta resist, and stitched with silk floss and very fine silk thread. Designed and worked by Ros Chilcot* (PHOTOGRAPHY: ROS CHILCOT)

were then judged by eye to make up the patterns. I liked the effect and found that I could emphasise it by pulling the stitches slightly to disturb the surface of the material, rucking it to give an interesting texture. By this time a useful bank of ideas had accumulated and been explored.

However, it was a summer holiday in France on the Côte d'Azur which produced the next and final stage. Another still-life was set up here using a check picnic cloth, a vase, some grapes and vine leaves, and the atmosphere and light of this beautiful place created a particularly evocative background. I used watercolour and masking-fluid for one drawing and pastels for another, and made several sketches of the leaves and grapes: I had a definite preference for the freedom of the watercolour, and the exercise gave me sufficient ideas to bring home ready to start the main embroidery.

A series of washes on thick silk twill, each using a silk dye with gutta as a resist, produced a free, spontaneous painting. After preparing the background, fabric areas were stitched, patterning freely by eye and using a flowing running stitch for a darning effect. Silk dyes on silk will retain the iridescent quality of the fabric, and the silk threads used for the embroidery enhanced the surface further. The original subject matter has therefore been retained, but reinterpreted in a contemporary and personal way.

The exploration of various drawing and painting media can be fun, and can help to decide which is the most effective. Similarly, trying out a stitch or technique in a traditional manner is an excellent way to understand it, before extending its use by varying size, shape or texture. The 'rules' that apply to traditional techniques can be broken with exciting effect.

Madeleine Clifton also broke the rules of her time, when most other embroiderers were filling spaces in an uninspired way and merely reproducing the designs of others with little or no originality, albeit with great skill. Today it is expected that creativity in embroidery and textiles should involve a questioning of those dogmatic pronouncements which imply only one correct way of working a technique. There is plenty of room for everyone's ideas to flourish, and for work to live in its own time *and* to develop in an innovative and interesting way.

CHAPTER ELEVEN

FOR YOUR DELIGHT

Dorothy Tucker

THE THREE BIRDS on a round stand shown here were made by Winsome Douglass in 1952 for the Needlework Development Scheme. Although the piece was intended as a toy to delight young people, it is in fact more essentially a visual aid, made with the aims of the scheme in mind, that is to increase design consciousness and raise standards in embroidery.

Made from commercially produced and dyed cottons, and embroidered with stranded cotton, it illustrates how inexpensive fabrics and threads can be used to good effect. The birds show how it is possible to build upon simple foundation shapes: the yellow bird is made from only the basic shape, while wings have been added to the grey one and the red bird has a comb and tail as well as wings. It is interesting to note the way in which the embroidered patterns fit decoratively into the shapes, rather than imitating the markings of recognisable birds or even feathers.

Winsome Douglass wrote a book entitled *Toys For Your Delight*, published by Mills and Boon in 1957, in which all the toys illustrated were designed and made by her. This is borne out by her detailed descriptions and in the way she anticipated practical problems in her instructions. She gave patterns and design ideas for almost every kind of animal or bird, carefully graded, starting from the very simplest and progressing to more elaborate ones. Sheets of drawings entitled 'Some Beaks and Bird Heads' or 'Bird Wings and More Bird Wings' and 'Some Ways of Making Bird Legs' were intended as stepping stones towards designing for oneself. The book provides

Decorative stitches: *a) stem b) back stitch, threaded c) back stitch, whipped d) running stitch, whipped e) buttonhole f) buttonhole variation g) buttonhole, knotted h) chain stitch, detached i) chain stitch j) feather k) single feather l) fly m) coral knot n) French knot o) single fly p) herringbone*

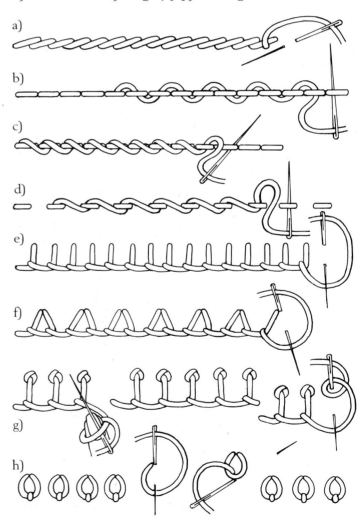

valuable clues as to the probable working methods used for the Embroiderers' Guild piece.

A simple side-view drawing of a bird was made and cut out from the drawing paper. A gusset was cut to fit, and shapes were cut for the wings, legs and combs. The base was planned and paper patterns made.

Fabrics were selected from a collection of scraps, and the paper shapes were placed on the straight grain of the fabric to avoid distortions later when assembling and stuffing. The pattern shapes were cut out of the fabric to include a seam allowance on all edges.

The fabric pieces were tacked over the paper patterns with the turnings to the wrong side, using a

Paper pattern for the bird
(DRAWINGS: MOLLIE PICKEN)

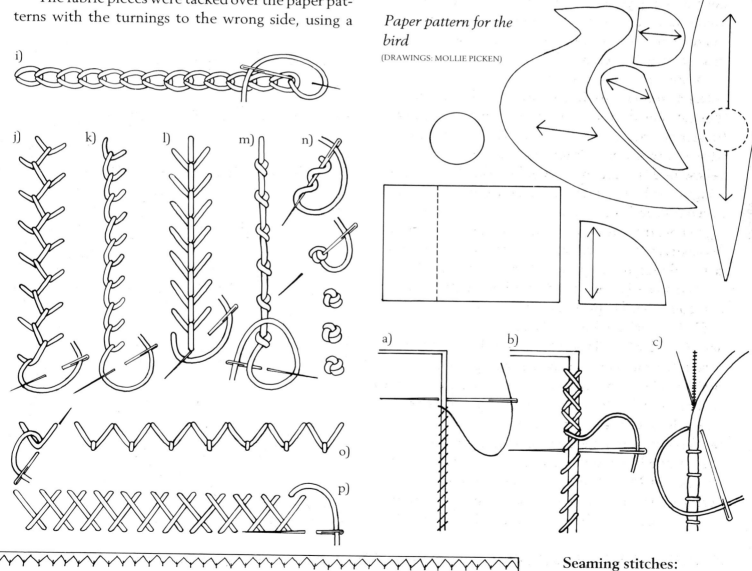

Seaming stitches:
a) *seaming on right side*
b) *crossed oversewing*
c) *couching over a seam*

69

Three birds on a round stand made by Winsome Douglass
EG no 1389; base, 15cm (6in); birds, 10cm (4in) high; and given by the Needlework Development Scheme in 1962 (PHOTOGRAPHY: DUDLEY MOSS)

(right) *Stitch samples in stranded cottons*
(PHOTOGRAPHY: DOROTHY TUCKER)

very fine needle and thread so that no holes showed when the tacking was removed. The fabric would have been clipped to ease the turnings around inside curves and points so that it would lie flat without bulges or wrinkles. The paper was not removed but left to give extra body and to help keep a firm shape.

The shapes were decorated with embroidered patterns stitched right through the paper. The designs may have been drawn freely onto the fabric with tailor's chalk, or drawn around solid cut-out shapes. Sometimes Winsome Douglass used to dot out the design with a sharp pencil or stylo. She points

The finished slippers in handmade felt, with stitchery worked in a variety of cotton and silk threads. A strip of cotton lawn was used to bind the edges. Shoe linings, covered and quilted, were used for the soles. Designed and worked by Dorothy Tucker
(PHOTOGRAPHY: DOROTHY TUCKER)

out that it is important to begin, and end, the embroidery well, and to avoid knots or long threads between rows on the back of the work. (If the stuffing lodges itself around them, this can pull and pucker the stitching.)

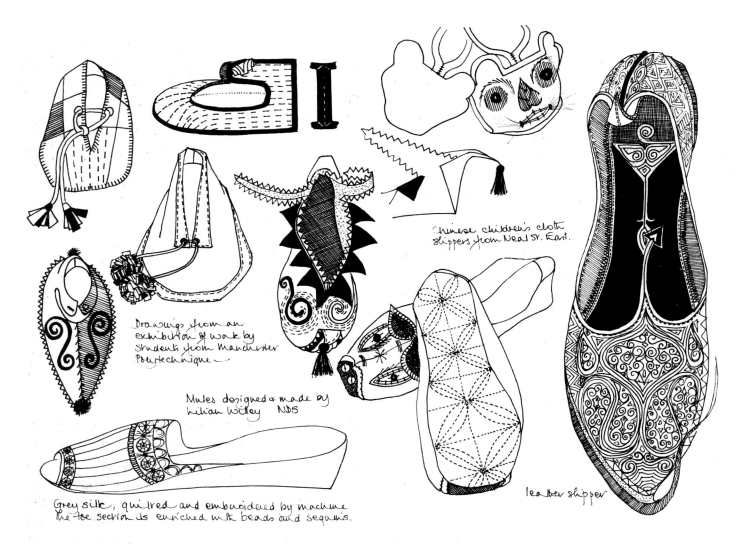

Drawings from an exhibition of work by students from Manchester Polytechnique

Mules designed & made by Lilian Witley NDS

Grey silk, quilted and embroidered by machine the toe section is enriched with beads and sequins.

Chinese children's cloth slippers from Neal St. East.

leather slipper

A sheet of drawings with spirals and serrated edges inspired by a collection of fabric shoes designed and made by a student from Manchester Polytechnic
(DRAWINGS: DOROTHY TUCKER)

When the embroidered designs were almost complete, the pieces were assembled and joined together in sequence. In this case, because the birds were small, the stitching was on the right side. Seaming stitch was used to give a firm, neat edge and each bird was stuffed firmly with kapok. The gaps were stitched up, and the final touches added. Winsome Douglass knew that toys tend to take on a life of their own, and for this reason left the eyes to the end.

The base was made with wood covered with fabric, with three holes drilled out to take the legs each bird stood on. These were short lengths of fabric-covered dowelling, measured and cut so they would stand upright and secure in the holes. Strengthened and neatened with closely worked buttonhole stitch, the legs were oversewn to the body of the bird.

The variety of stitches and the contrasts in tone and colour in the illustrated example are typical of the items made for the Needlework Development Scheme which was formed in 1934 to stimulate an interest in embroidery and to raise standards of design. With this in mind a collection of historical and foreign embroidery was built up and circulated to teachers and students to study first hand. From 1948–50 Ulla Kockum, a designer from Sweden, was 'expert in charge'. She introduced a number of Swedish embroideries into the collection.

Swedish peasant embroidery was made for everyday use or festive occasions. Traditional designs were usually based on flowers, animals and birds. They had a certain spontaneity and were worked on hand-woven fabrics with home-dyed yarns. These qualities were lost with industrialisation. In 1894, inspired by the William Morris Movement, a handful of people formed 'Foreningen Handarbetets Vanner' (the friends of weaving and needlework). Their aim was to restore typically Swedish design. At first they turned to the Vikings for inspiration but when this did not suit the decoration of nineteenth-century homes other sources were found. During the 1930s striking modern designs from Sweden were seen in England. When it became apparent to the NDS that contemporary work held more appeal, a number of contemporary collections were made specifically for schools.

The NDS also produced books and regular bulletins, for example *And So to Sew* and *So to Embroider* which can still sometimes be found in workroom cupboards or neglected shelves. Winsome Douglass made many visual aids for the NDS, and wrote a number of books. Her work is characterised by a strong sense of design, matched with an ability to choose and use a variety of embroidery stitches in very expressive and decorative ways. The Embroiderers' Guild Collection contains several examples of her work. When considering this piece as a source of inspiration, it was no surprise to find that the illustrations in Winsome Douglass's book had been traced off by previous readers. The pages were indented with their pencils!

Thoughts about following a bird theme or making another toy were discarded but other ideas lingered, such as embroidered patterns across a patchwork of printed fabrics in NDS style or, in contrast, white stitchery surrounding applied shapes with the design of a lizard. Then a collection of fabric shoes designed and made by a student from Manchester Polytechnic inspired a sheet of drawings with spirals and serrated edges.

The decision to make a pair of mules was made as a result of seeing the lizard design and a drawing of an Indian slipper together. A simple pattern was then made from Vilene (Pellon) and the lizard placed in different positions, as it was not just a matter of designing one shoe but a pair to be worn together. There were many constructional and technical problems to be solved which were tackled through a series of tests. The warm, soft, handmade felt quilted readily, and was compatible with a lizard applied in red felted flannel; the flannel cut beautifully to give clean, non-fraying edges. A single strand

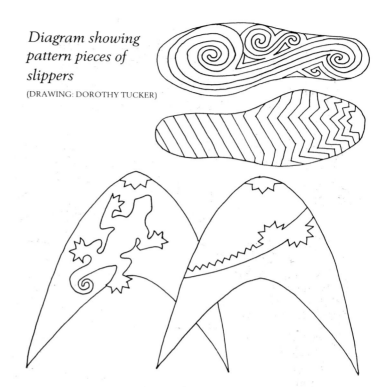

Diagram showing pattern pieces of slippers
(DRAWING: DOROTHY TUCKER)

of silk weaving yarn proved to be the right weight for the embroidery and combined well with other coloured cotton and silk threads. A strip of cotton lawn cut on the bias and sewn to bind the edges of the shapes was the solution to the problem of neatening and joining the pieces together; further, its stripy print determined the colours to be used. Shoe linings, covered and quilted, were used for the soles.

When it came to the embroidery, the whole process slowed down since it involved going backwards to learn and get into the rhythm of the stitches Winsome Douglass had used. With two strands of stranded cotton throughout, her work was perfectly evenly spaced, each stitch a clear mark linking almost mathematically into the next. The discovery that crossed Van Dyke stitch moves easily around curves and makes marvellous spiky spirals was the reward for doing a sampler as near to the original as possible.

Winsome Douglass's birds lack the expressive spontaneity of either childrens' work or peasant art, and in the same way these slippers are also 'designed' items. The use of handmade felt and Vilene (Pellon) is a move forward from the craft felt and paper of 'The Fifties', and the spiky spirals of crossed Van Dyke stitch embedded in the handmade felt have great potential for further contemporary work.

CHAPTER TWELVE

A QUILTED FRAGMENT

Jenny Bullen

THE FRAGMENT illustrated here measures 36 x 17.5cm (14 x 7in) and although it is not dated, it probably originates from the mid- to late seventeenth century. It is worked in a combination of flat and corded quilting with added surface stitchery, a technique that was very popular in the seventeenth century. The fragment has not been re-assembled in any way, nor does it appear to have been repaired or conserved. The top fabric has worn away in several places but the stitchery is remarkably intact.

Bed quilts using this technique were made throughout the century, but this fragment appears to be part of a garment, its unusual shape giving the impression of a piece cut from an item of clothing. (Quilted clothing was very popular at this time.) The quilting was often combined with other types of embroidery, as shown here, and the embroidery would form the dominant part of the design, usually of large stylised flowers, with the background covered in corded quilting, often in geometric patterns. As well as the floral designs there might be smaller geometric patterns, usually embroidered in self-coloured thread whose main function appeared to be to fill any unworked areas of cloth.

The embroidery design on the fragment is of various large floral patterns, the long, curving stems of the flowers serving to join them all together. They are somewhat reminiscent of the patterns on the chintzes brought into the country from the East: the East India Company was formed in 1600 and imported a great many fabrics and textiles into England from the Orient; these designs greatly influenced contemporary embroidery.

There is no record of the embroiderer with the fragment. However, the very high standard of workmanship leads us to the possible assumption that it

was the work of professional quilters, or that the pattern was drawn out by professional pattern makers. A seventeenth-century waistcoat illustrated in Averil Colby's book *Quilting* is inscribed thus: 'John Stilwell, Drawear, at ye Flaming Toorch in Russel Street Cou(rt)'.

(above) *Detail of stitching*   (PHOTOGRAPHY: DUDLEY MOSS)

(right) *Quilted fragment; probably from a seventeenth-century garment, it is worked in a combination of flat and corded quilting with added surface embroidery. Although it is a fragment and looks very fragile, this impression is in fact misleading as the piece is in remarkably good condition*
EG no 4642; 36 x 17.5cm (14¼ x 7in); given by
John Jacobie   (PHOTOGRAPHY: DUDLEY MOSS)

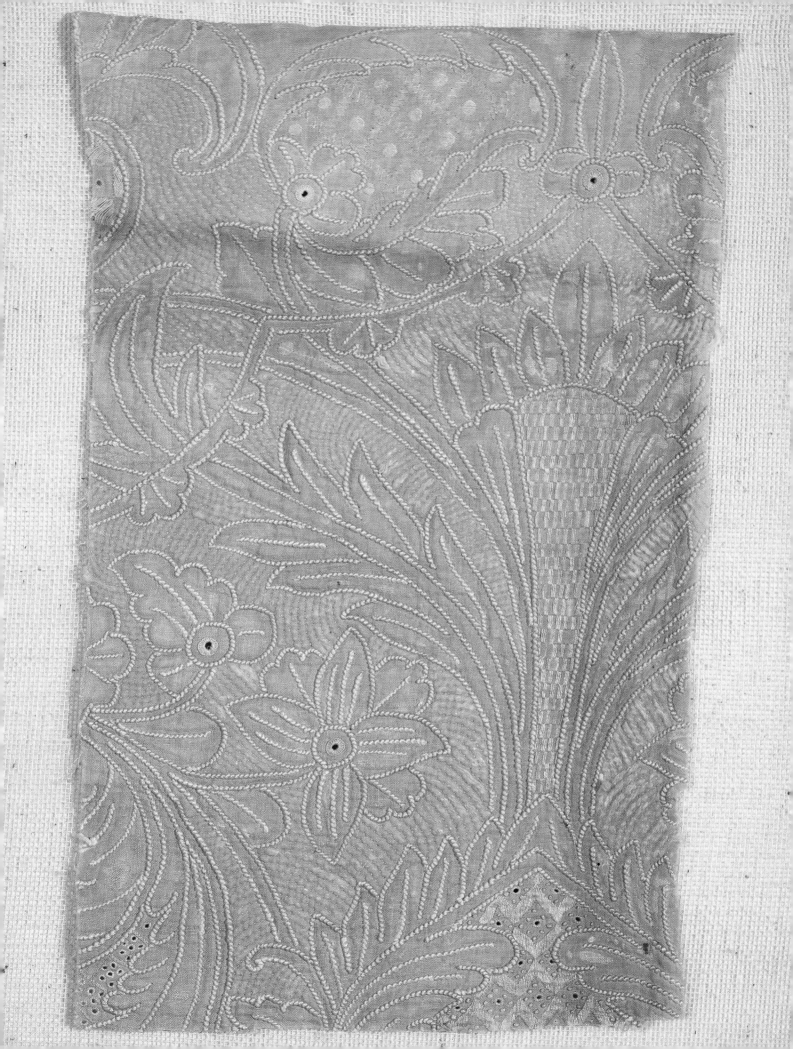

The top fabric is fine cotton, and a coarser linen has been used for the backing. The top fabric and the threads are a pale tea colour, very patchy and faded in areas. On inspection of the reverse of the fabric, however, both the linen and the embroidery threads are seen to be natural coloured, leading to the supposition that the piece was dyed or painted with colour, possibly at a later date. However, Mrs Colby states that some of the threads used at that time were often coloured, though would fade to the natural state with age. The top fabric has worn away in places to reveal the backing fabric. The corded areas are very dense – in some places the wool shows through the top fabric.

A thick silk thread has been used for the floral embroidery, and a very fine thread, either silk or cotton, for the spot patterns and the cording stitch. Fine wool has been used to thread through the corded areas. Whether the original fabric was coloured or in its natural state, the threads were carefully chosen to match the colour of the ground fabric. Outline stitch has been used for the large floral shapes, and other embroidery stitches were used for the designs inside the leaves and flowers. Blocks of satin stitch in a fine thread have been worked inside one of the large shapes. In another part of the design, herringbone stitch and tiny circles of satin stitch have been used for an infilling pattern. Circles of tiny buttonhole stitch, combined with French knots, have been embroidered in the centres of some of the flowers. The channels for the corded quilting are worked in tiny running stitches.

The design was probably marked on the top fabric using the prick and pounce method, although there are no visible marking lines on the fragment. It is unlikely that templates were used because of the complexity of the design. The two layers of fabric were tacked together and the surface embroidery stitches worked with the smaller, spot patterns next in sequence. Finally, the cording threads were inserted through the stitched channels. While researching and writing about the original embroidery, consideration was given to the contemporary work to be developed from the fragment. The original design is very formal and stylised and initially I thought that this might pose a problem when translating it to

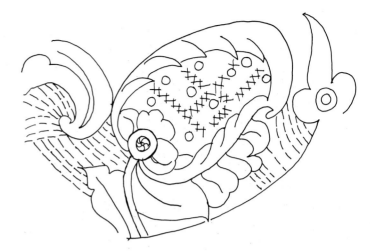

Diagram showing one of the stylised flowers. A pattern of satin stitch spots, and rows of herringbone stitch can be seen in the centre of the leaf

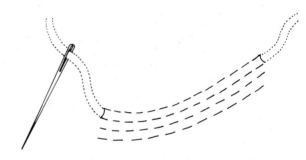

Corded quilting: the channels are stitched through the top and backing fabrics using either tiny running or back stitches. A thick yarn, usually wool, is then threaded through each channel in turn
(DRAWINGS: MOLLIE PICKEN)

a twentieth-century embroidery. At the same time I considered it very important to retain the fragile, almost transparent, ethereal feel of the fragment.

Some quick colour sketches using water-soluble crayons were made of the stylised flowers, in an attempt to convey this fragility. An attempt was also made to obtain the same colours as the original. These sketches were pinned to the wall and left for some time before any decision was made as to the final appearance of the embroidery.

I eventually decided to keep to the original design of the stylised flowers, and to include the spot patterns and the patterns made by the channels of the corded quilting, which in themselves presented another area of study.

A piece of fine silk chiffon was chosen as the top

Two or more small experiments using paper, with machine-stitched channels. The surfaces were coloured and waxed. On one piece couched metal threads have been added, and on the second, running stitches in a coarse thread
(PHOTOGRAPHY: JIM PASCOE)

CHAPTER THIRTEEN

THE MATYO ROSE

Diana Keay

MEZOKOVESD is a small country town attractively situated north-east of Budapest, at the base of mountains which rise from the Hungarian Plain. The area is known as the Matyo area, and incorporates two nearby villages. Today, Mezokovesd is served by a railway from Budapest; and in the town is the Matyo Museum and the Matyo Co-operative for embroidery and craft.

The fragment illustrated is made from a manufactured cream-coloured cotton cambric which has been closely embroidered in bright colours, allowing little of the background to show. The design consists of six different flower motifs ranging from approximately 7–4cm (2¾–1½in) in diameter which are closely arranged along each length of the fragment. Between these two borders there is a trail of rosebuds together with leaf spray. In the intervening spaces, daisy-like flowers with five petals are placed. The whole fragment is embroidered in floss silk, in satin stitch with just a very small amount of stem stitch in the following colours: scarlet and wine red; orange and burnt orange; pale yellow and gold; pale pink and cerise; magenta; pale blue and dark blue; and blue-green in two tones. The colours of the floss silk are very bright, suggesting that they were chemically dyed. The satin stitch is closely worked right through the fabric which makes the piece almost reversible. The direction of the satin stitch varies according to the shape of the flower motif, with the floss silk giving a rippled effect. Some of the embroidery stitching, especially those small areas worked in pale blue silk, appears to have been taken out, as there are needle holes showing where the close stitches were formerly worked. This also reveals the design which was apparently drawn in pencil.

Most of the fragment is in very good condition, and the colours of the embroidery threads show no fading. The whole fragment has been faced with a beige bias binding to protect the edges, but unfortunately this cuts through the design in places. There are no joins, and it appears to have been worked in the home by one person.

The embroidery from Mezokovesd could have been either from the sleeve of a man's shirt (such sleeves were extremely wide and were decorated at the wrist end), or from a bed sheet (sheets with decorated borders were used as bed covers in the traditional peasant home). Dr Hankoczi Gyula of the Matyo Museum in Mezokovesd states that the embroidery on a sleeve would be part of that sleeve, whereas the embroidery for a sheet consisted of a strip which was applied, there being two parts, each 55–60cm (21½–23½in) wide. It is difficult to examine this piece because the edges have been faced with a binding, as already mentioned. It is dated to the 1920s or 1930s.

Embroidery was traditionally worked in the home in Mezokovesd, even in times of hardship; and although some peasants were prosperous, many were very poor. Whatever her status, every mother aimed to supply her daughter with a dowry consisting of enough clothes for her lifetime, and household linen – the most important items being the embroidered pillows and sheets. At the turn of the century, when the men had to seek work away from the town, the women supplemented their income by making and selling specially embroidered items.

Hungarian embroidery is divided into two groups: the earlier geometrical, and freehand. In Mezokovesd, the design on this fragment can be traced back to the 'Old' style, which showed stylised flower clusters and a scroll, worked symmetrically on

One of the Matyo roses (left) *taken from the apron. This shape, together with its details, suggested a bag with leather, beads and quilting, as shown on the right*

(DRAWING: MILLIE PICKEN)

☐ leather

☐ beads

—— quilting outline

a sheet border in red and blue cotton. Later, the 'New' or 'Peasant' style showed the design executed asymmetrically, in a freehand way, with the flower clusters becoming 'roses' and intertwined, this time, with a scroll with leaves, still worked in red and blue. Later in the nineteenth century, the same design with 'roses' (now called the 'Matyo rose') was worked in either wool, silk or artificial silk or cotton, in brilliant colours, obviously chemically dyed. It featured not only on shirt sleeves and sheets as covers, but on other articles, especially the festival apron worn by young men and girls. The fragment here under examination, dated to after World War I, belongs to the 'Latest' style and shows the continuation of the 'Matyo rose' design.

The embroiderer would probably buy the cambric and threads in the market. Next she would need to decide on a design, which would be traditional to her, having evolved through the centuries. Perhaps she would seek help from someone skilled in this field. There was such a person in Mezokovesd, namely Kis Janko Bori (1876–1954) who embroidered and drew patterns in the Matyo style and was

instrumental in founding the Matyo Co-operative, in 1951.

To transfer the design, the embroiderer drew it onto the cambric with a pencil, or used a template for the larger motifs, filling in the smaller details freehand. Whichever method was employed, she was able to begin embroidering in satin stitch, choosing her colours from the traditional spectrum.

After visiting Hungary my lasting impressions were of the peaceful and unsophisticated countryside contrasting with the lively music and dancing, and the colourful costume of the people. The young man's festival apron is a typical example of the latter, and became the inspiration for the embroidered bag shown here. As embroidery in Hungary is used for a purpose, it seemed appropriate to make an object for specific use on special occasions.

The first thought was to include a macramé fringe as on the original, but the effect was overpowering on a smaller piece so a decorative tassel was used instead.

The colour red was chosen to suggest Hungary and roses, and the bag is made of red silk which was

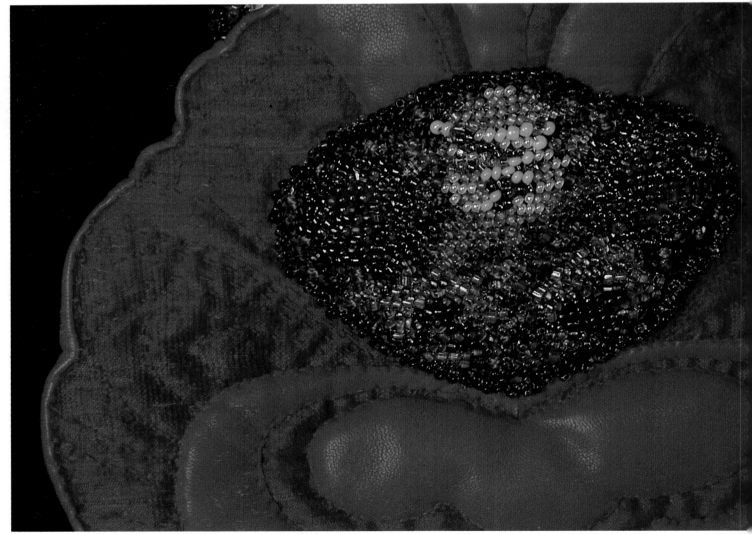

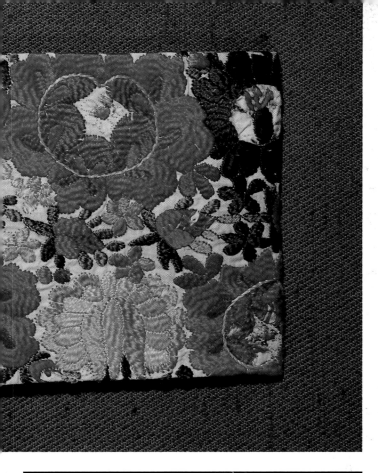

quilted on the front and back. Appliqué using leather was incorporated, as it was reminiscent of other Hungarian embroideries. Beads suggested an alternative to the heavy satin stitches, and a motif was worked on no 10 double canvas. This was cut out and applied to the front flap of the bag, and gave a rich textured quality to the finished appearance.

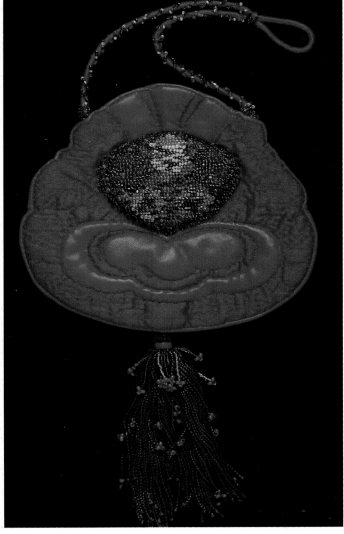

(top left) *Part of a Hungarian shirt sleeve or sheet made from a manufactured cream-coloured cotton cambric, closely embroidered in bright colours. The whole fragment is embroidered in floss silk, in satin stitch, with just a very small amount of stem stitch EG no 2251; 1920s or 30s* (PHOTOGRAPHY: DUDLEY MOSS)

(far left) *Detail of finished bag, showing the beaded motif. Designed and worked by Diana Keay* (PHOTOGRAPHY: JIM PASCOE)

(left) *The completed bag is made of red quilted silk with applied leather shapes and beadwork inset, and completed with a decorative handle and tassels. Designed and worked by Diana Keay* (PHOTOGRAPHY: JIM PASCOE)

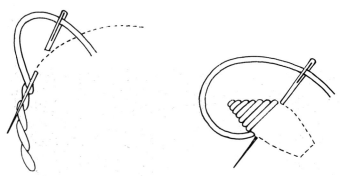

Stem stitch worked with thread above the needle to form a curve, and a block of satin stitch

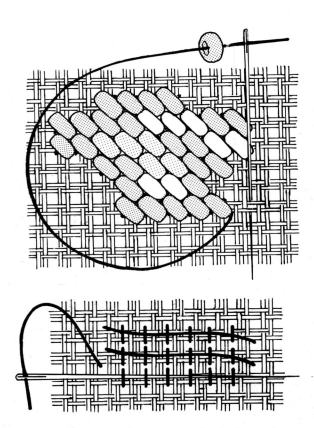

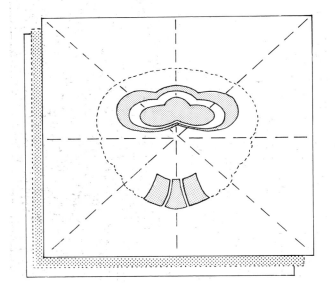

Front and back view showing method of attaching beads to double canvas

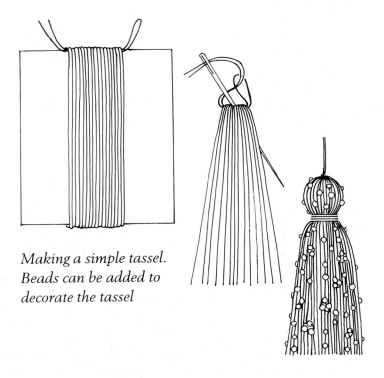

Making a simple tassel. Beads can be added to decorate the tassel

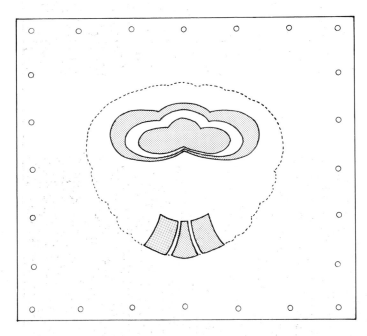

Stages in quilting showing the layers of leather, silk and wadding (DRAWINGS: MOLLIE PICKEN)

(right) *Drawing of the Hungarian apron*
(DRAWING: MOLLIE PICKEN)

CHAPTER FOURTEEN

PATTERNS FROM NAXOS

Vicky Lugg

THE EARLY seventeenth-century cushion panel from the Greek Island of Naxos illustrated here, is embroidered in a simple, closely worked darning stitch on an unbleached linen homespun fabric. Soft, lustrous, slightly twisted silk threads in contrasting, vibrant colours are used for the embroidery. The silk thread is at times used both horizontally and vertically, giving an apparent change of colour as the light plays on the surface. Judging by an unfinished sample, the design would have been drawn onto the back of the material and embroidered from the wrong side. Most of the darning is worked parallel with the weft threads and the embroidery is worked backwards and forwards across a motif in a continuous movement. The large medallions are worked in two sections, with the centre diamond being stitched separately from the border. There is no apparent join in the thread on the right side of the work.

The principal colour is a rusty red with subtle variations of colour and tone; there are also blue threads, but these appear to be more faded and worn than the red, which could possibly be the result of the natural dyeing process.

The piece has been conserved by mounting it on hexagonal net. It is lightly attached with lines of long tacking stitches, and areas that are split or worn are strengthened by lightweight muslin. An attempt has been made at some time to mend a large hole of 2 x 3.5cm (3/4 x 1 1/4in) with a coarse thread, worked in a form of detached buttonhole stitch.

It is easy to imagine how rich and sumptuous this large silk and linen cushion cover would look in the clear, bright light of the Greek Islands and in the surroundings of a simple, whitewashed village house. The cushion was almost certainly embroidered as part of a girl's dowry, one of many articles

that she would have worked herself, as part of her marriage contract. (This ancient tradition died out in the late nineteenth century.) The dowry would have included a number of embroidered dresses and household furnishings, including those for the marriage bed, and would have been displayed at the

(above) *Detail of cushion panel*   (PHOTOGRAPHY: DUDLEY MOSS)

(right) *Early seventeenth-century cushion panel, from Naxos, Greek Islands. The embroidery is worked in a simple darning stitch using soft silk threads on an unbleached linen homespun fabric. The principal colour is a rusty red with subtle variations of colour and tone EG no 4931; 102.5 x 47cm(40 1/4 x 18 1/2in); given by Miss Beale*   (PHOTOGRAPHY: DUDLEY MOSS)

wedding and other festivals. The bed was often a simple raised platform (or an alcove in the single living-room) similar to a box bed, piled with cushions or pillows, and with hangings for privacy. Long cushions would have been used on a Turkish-style divan in the living-room. All these hangings and covers were embroidered in styles specific to each island, and the importance of the embroideries in domestic life is emphasised by frequent reference to them in traditional songs and in stories which were handed down from generation to generation.

The origins of this beautiful embroidery lie deep in the rich and ever-changing history of the eastern Mediterranean. The island of Naxos is one of the Greek Cycladic islands, which are scattered across the Aegean Sea to the east of mainland Greece. The designs differ from island to island and are the result of influences from the Byzantine, Venetian and Turkish cultures. Motifs were developed from plant, flower, animal and bird forms becoming in some cases so formalised and simplified that any representational character is lost. This is particularly true of the geometric designs of Naxos, which form all-over repeat patterns. This stylisation of natural form is usual in peasant embroidery, and the embroidery of the Greek Islands is essentially a peasant art. Geometric patterns have always been a popular source of design, but the developments christened by scholars the 'King' pattern and the 'Naxos Star' give a particular character to this embroidery.

Design work based on tracings from photographs of the original textile
(PHOTOGRAPHY: JIM PASCOE)

The tradition of creating embroidered furnishings for household use flourished in the seventeenth and eighteenth centuries, but declined during the nineteenth for political and commercial reasons. It is suggested that the decline of silk production on the islands deprived the workers of their raw materials, and that the islanders preferred the cheaper manufactured woven silk produced after the introduction of the power loom in western Europe. Since no new embroideries were created, the old ones were handed down from one generation to the next, although not always in their entirety as larger items were cut up to subscribe to the traditional form of dowry.

The large collection of Greek Island embroideries available for study in the United Kingdom is due to the interest and appreciation of visitors to Greece. It is even more fortunate that amongst them were a number of scholars from the British School of Archaeology in Athens, who treated the subject as a serious study and amassed rich collections, providing documentation which has proved a reliable guide in the attributing of the embroideries.

The famous red embroidery from Naxos appears to have been made in enormous quantities, and is unlike embroidery from other islands in that the whole surface is covered with a repeating design which is derived from the double-leaf 'King' pattern. In most cases the soft silk embroidery thread dominates the surface of the undyed homespun linen or

Patterns and tone worked freely with brush-marks using watercolour paint
(PHOTOGRAPHY: JIM PASCOE)

cotton, and this thread is invariably red with the occasional addition of blue. All the silk used in the old embroideries was dyed locally with vegetable dyes, which gave wonderful soft, subtle variations to the clear red.

My first impressions of the cushion panel were dominated by the movement of colour and pattern across the surface of the textile. The colour move-ment is created by the stitch direction of the thick floss silk, and the pattern movement by the subtle changes produced by the positive and negative shapes in the design. In order to explore these impressions a series of tracings of various motifs was made from photographs of the original textile. The contrast of scale and overlap of patterns created in this way suggested further possible developments, one of which was to work into the traced design with wax crayon resist and watercolour paint. Other methods of recording the patterns included torn paper collage, watercolour painting, and simple mono-printing with custom-made blocks. The printing in particular highlighted the contrast of the positive and negative aspects of the original design. In the original, the light-coloured background fabric at times looks as if it is printed on the darker surface of the embroidery, and this suggested further designs that could be used for embroidery.

The vibrant contrast of the thread colours in the original piece was so exciting that I decided to use similar colours for the contemporary work, and selected a variety of threads to work with. A natural linen scrim was dyed for the background, and a basic overall design of the various motifs was printed on the dyed linen with an opaque fabric paint. The patterns created on paper were used as a guide. The scrim was backed by calico to give a firmer surface for stitching, and the design was developed with hand-stitching and appliqué, emphasising certain areas of colour, texture and structure to contrast with the softer colours and less defined patterns of other parts of the surface. The edges of the scrim were frayed and left unfinished, echoing the quality of the original fabric.

(left) *Printing blocks were used to print an image in masking fluid, protecting the background papers as well as an image in opaque paint* (PHOTOGRAPHY: JIM PASCOE)

(right) *Patterns from Naxos. Dyed linen scrim embroidered with linen, cotton and silk in a variety of straight stitches and French knots. Applied materials are dyed organzas and handmade paper. Designed and worked by Vicky Lugg* (PHOTOGRAPHY: JIM PASCOE)

CHAPTER FIFTEEN

CASAL GUIDI EMBROIDERY

Muriel Fry

THE TWO BAGS illustrated are worked in a type of embroidery called Casal Guidi work. Casal Guidi is a village near Pistoia, north-east of Florence, and it gave its name to a style of embroidery of the late nineteenth and early twentieth centuries. This period saw a revival of a number of traditional Italian whitework techniques including reticella, punto in aria, filet and richelieu work. The revivals differed from their historical counterparts in that a much coarser weight of linen or cotton fabric and thread was used, and that the techniques were employed on decorative articles such as garments or furnishings.

The larger of the two bags illustrated shows a heraldic design of a pair of winged griffins drinking at a central fountain. Worked in detached buttonhole stitch, the bodies are firmly stuffed with scraps of fabric; the wings, beaks and tails are sewn in whipped stem stitch and buttonhole loops. The smaller bag has a stylised floral motif worked in

Bobble: *For best results use a firmly twisted thread and a tapestry needle. It is essential to work a sample to gauge both the size of bobble required and the length of thread needed. A continuous thread will avoid the need for awkward joins*

a) Form a small ring of thread, leaving the tail free and securing the ring with a twisted buttonhole stitch

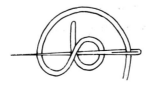

b,c) Continue making 8–10 twisted buttonhole stitches into the ring.

d) Pull the trail of thread tight to close the ring and secure it with a back stitch. Do not cut the tail off but secure it within the ball

e) Continue working twisted buttonhole stitches into the spaces in previous rows

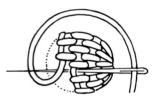

f) After two or three rows, stuff the ball with a scrap of fabric or thread and continue stitching to cover. Pull the last few stitches tightly to close the top of the ball. Secure the thread with a back stitch and use the end to attach the ball

(DRAWINGS: MOLLIE PICKEN)

Single Italian insertion stitch: *This is a variation of Italian buttonhole stitch (Mary Thomas' Dictionary of Stitches) but with only one buttonhole stitch being worked over each side loop, creating a lacy,*

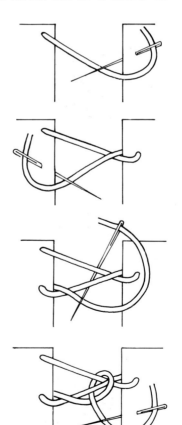

open effect. A firmly twisted thread should be used

detached buttonhole stitch, whipped stem stitch and raised stem band. Both bags fasten with a drawstring and bobble tassels decorate the base.

In Italy, not only did the leisured lady work embroidery of this kind for her own use, but, as in parts of Britain, sewing industries creating employment were established. Visitors to Italy bought examples of Casal Guidi work from that produced by a skilled workforce trained in a special school in the village. Some of these pieces have found their way into British collections; there are twelve pieces in the Embroiderers' Guild Collection.

The elaborate decoration of these small, unlined, flat bags, purses or sachets is usually only on the front, and the two sections of the bags are hemstitched fabrics, joined by insertion stitches. Designs are arranged symmetrically, some covering the whole of the front but, more usually, forming a band towards the lower edge of the bag or flap of a

purse. Cushion covers and table-mats were made with Casal Guidi borders.

In general a white or natural linen fabric, not strictly evenweave, is stitched with a matching thread, though occasionally a coloured linen is used with natural coloured embroidery. The technique consists of a pulled work ground in four-sided stitch supporting heavily padded and detached surface stitchery. Often two weights of linen thread are used, coarser for the surface stitchery and finer for the pulled work ground, insertion seams and buttonhole loop fastenings.

A strong feature of all Casal Guidi bags is the decorative trimmings and fastenings. Fingercord drawstrings are carried either in a row of vertical buttonhole bars just below the top opening or through half-circle loops along the top edge. The latter carry a series of complex picots, making a beautiful decoration reminiscent of a coronet. They

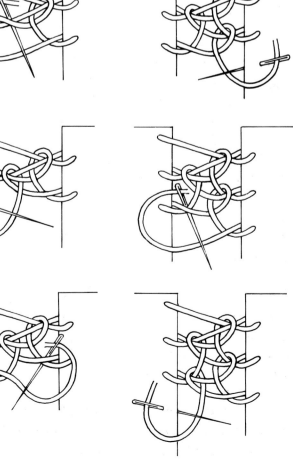

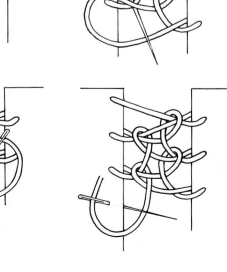

Coronet picot: *This picot can be worked into a base of fabric hem, a buttonhole bar or a thread ring. Use a firmly twisted thread. Work from right to left*

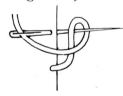

a) Secure thread at right of work and make a twisted buttonhole stitch into base. Pull firm

b) Make a buttonhole stitch into working thread close to base knot, pull into small knot

c) Make a second buttonhole stitch between the knot and the base stitch, pulling firm

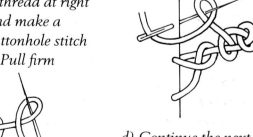

d) Continue the next picot a short distance from the first

(DRAWINGS: MOLLIE PICKEN)

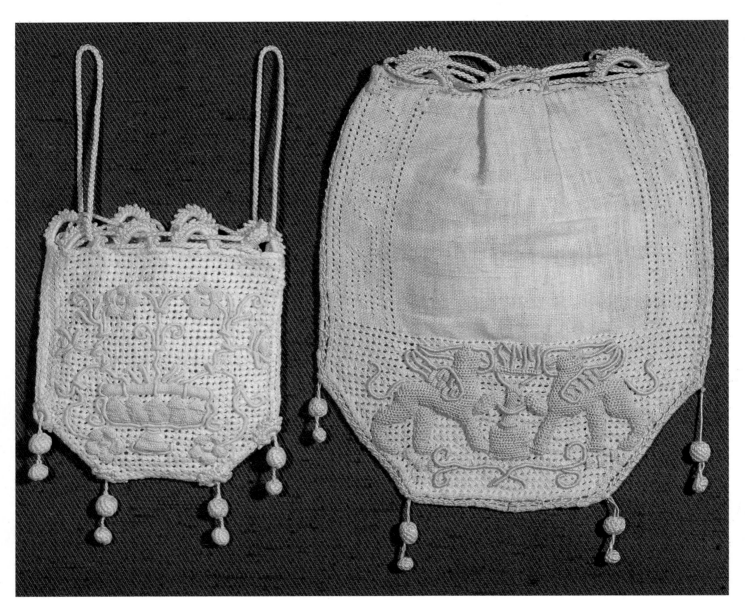

Two small, unlined, flat bags in Casal Guidi embroidery worked on a white or natural linen fabric and stitched with a matching thread. Both bags show simple paired bobbles, 4cm (1¹/₂in) long, 'coronet' picot loops and fingercord drawstrings
EG no 3493; 14cm (5¹/₂in) square; lent by Lady Bland
EG no 4889; 25 x 22.5cm (10 x 9in); given by Mrs Alexander (PHOTOGRAPHY: DUDLEY MOSS)

also occur as detached rings applied to the smaller bag in the photograph. In fact five forms of buttonhole stitch are used in the Casal Guidi bags, making a richly textured embroidery: detached padded buttonhole and buttonhole bars form plant and griffin motifs; buttonhole loops supporting coronet picots carry the drawstrings; twisted buttonhole makes the suspended bobbles; and buttonhole stitch is incorporated into the insertion seams joining back and front bag panels.

Tassels in a variety of designs give a weighted lower edge. Linked by a twisted thread, pairs of plain bobbles are made of buttonhole stitches padded with fabric scraps or wooden beads. These may be further embellished with whipped or buttonholed bars. Knotted threads are also used to make lively and unusual tassel trims.

The wealth of detailed trimmings on Casal Guidi work is of particular interest since this area of embroidery is often neglected. Details can be studied

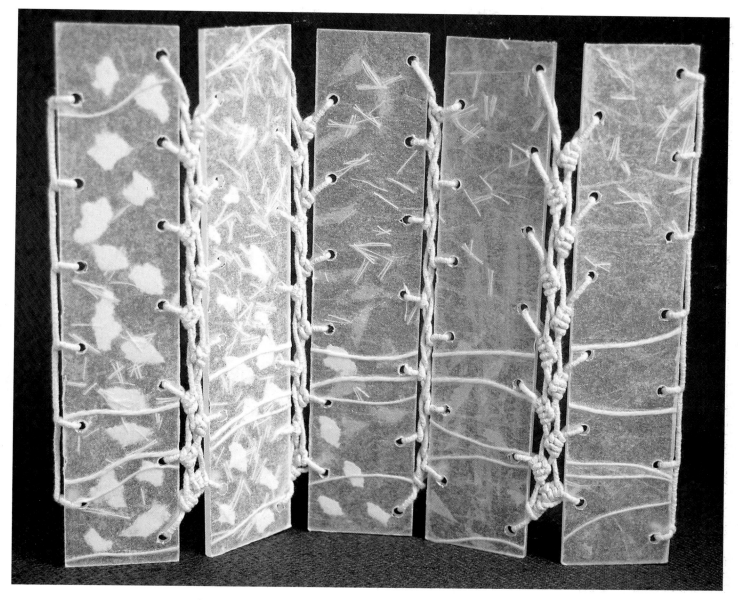

Maquette for a screen. Paper and thread collaged under tissue paper onto clear perspex. Varieties of Italian buttonhole insertions join the panels and act as hinges. 24.5 x 20cm (9³/₄ x 8in). Designed and worked by Muriel Fry (PHOTOGRAPHY: JIM S. FRASER)

under a magnifier, by taking close-up photographs or in some cases by making enlargements of the actual embroidery on a photocopier. Not only will construction methods then be more easily identified, but the enlargements themselves can act as inspiration for an exciting contemporary development. Stitches worked on a large scale take on a sculptural quality and can form the basis of an interesting study in themselves.

Insertion stitch is based on a simple cretan stitch, but after each stitch is made into the seam, a single buttonhole stitch is worked over the preceding one. The formation of Italian buttonhole insertion stitch has the same basic structure but with four buttonhole stitches over each cretan foundation stitch.

In the Casal Guidi examples the insertion stitches are fairly widely spaced, giving a beautiful lacy effect. To investigate the stitch structure without resorting to a magnifier, the stitch can be worked on a large scale; by using a variety of coarse threads, knitting yarns or cords on a rug canvas, for example, it takes on different decorative qualities. Experiments can be made with the aim of contrasting matt and shiny or crisp and hairy yarns, each of which will

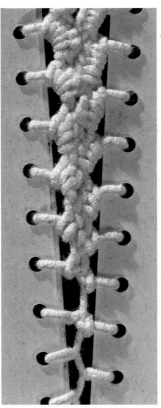

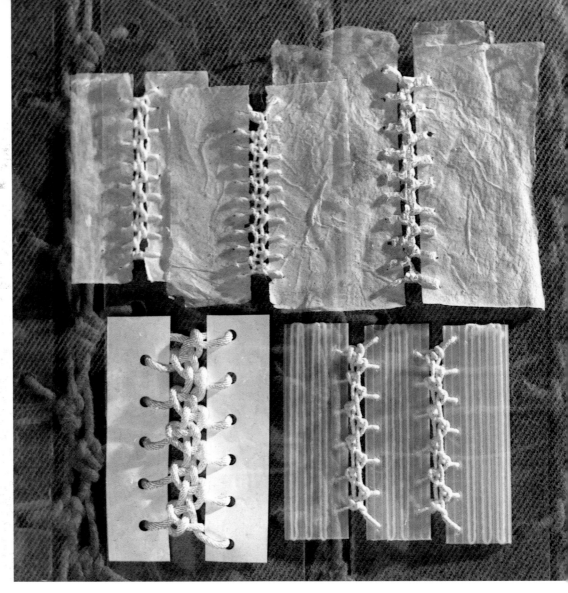

(left) *Graded insertion stitch increasing from cretan to Italian insertion with four buttonhole loops. Drilled clear perspex stitched with machine-whipped cord (25mm (1in) between holes). Graded insertion stitch increasing from cretan to Italian insertion with six buttonhole loops. Drilled clear perspex stitched with machine-whipped cord (12mm (1/2in) between holes)*
(PHOTOGRAPHY: JIM S. FRASER)

Experimental samples of single Italian insertion stitch using a variety of yarns and cords on handmade paper, card and reeded plastic (PHOTOGRAPHY: JIM S. FRASER)

give a different character to the same stitch. Changing the spacing, direction or tightness of working will add to the range of possible effects.

Italian buttonhole insertion stitches are normally worked between straight parallel seams. If a line of stitches is made, starting with simple cretan and adding progressively one, two, three and four buttonhole stitches, a gradually widening insertion results. A further variation might be combined with curving seams, and these could have a useful application as a method of creating shape within the structure of a garment or accessory.

Continuing the investigation into changes of scale and quality, I considered using materials such as paper, card, plastic, perspex and wood instead of fabric. To make it easier to stitch paper it was an advantage to stiffen it with PVA adhesive or iron-on

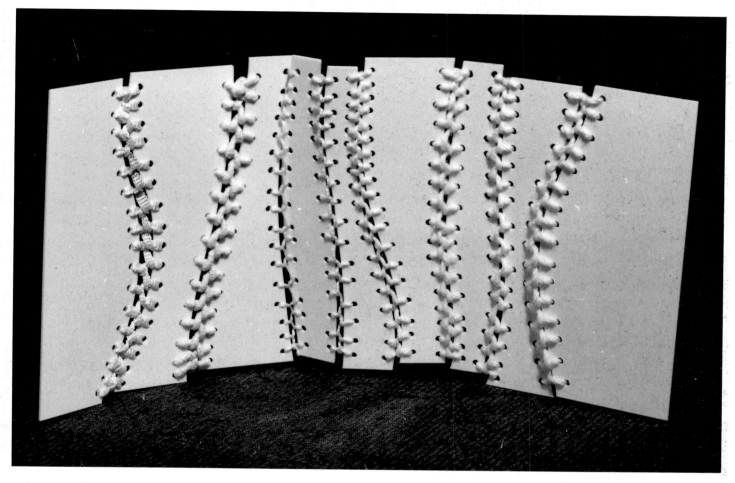

Vilene (Pellon) on the reverse. With some materials, however, it was necessary to punch or drill holes at appropriate spacings through which to stitch the thread.

In using these inflexible materials, the insertions formed a type of hinge, opening up the exciting possibility of three-dimensional forms. Screens or room-dividers in which the hinge stitches are an important decorative feature, proved an idea worth pursuing. In the illustrated maquette for a screen, panels of perspex have been textured and rendered opaque with thread and paper scraps collaged under tissue paper. Holes drilled at appropriate spacings carry buttonhole insertion stitches made of machine-whipped cords.

All these experimental variations are based on the investigation of a single stitch, proving that there is scope for a lifetime's research from the starting-point of simple, traditional stitches. In the button-hole stitches alone of Casal Guidi work, there remains a wealth of further creative possibilities.

(above) *Further experiments using curving seams*

(PHOTOGRAPHY: JIM S. FRASER)

(below) *Detail of maquette (30mm (1¹/₂in) between holes)*

(PHOTOGRAPHY: JIM S. FRASER)

CHAPTER SIXTEEN

PAGAN MYTHS IN EMBROIDERY

Anne Coleman

T HE EMBROIDERY illustrated here is probably
of peasant origin, worked in the first half
of the nineteenth century in a village in
the north-west of the former USSR, bordering
Finland.

Similar embroideries were worked in the region
south from Archangel to Novgarod, and have the
characteristic design motifs found in this area, not
only on textiles, but also in woodcarving, printing
and ceramics. The motifs on these designs probably
derived from an ancient pagan culture which included fertility rites and nature worship, for the symbols include the sun and moon, water, trees, animals
and birds, and huge, strange mythological figures,
some half human and half animal. The return of the
sun and the warmth of spring after the dark, cold
days of winter have always been a cause for great re-
joicing and thanksgiving to people living in the far
North.

Christianity only reached this area of Russia in
the tenth century, and pagan ideas were probably incorporated into the new religion in the same way as
trees, eggs, birds and animals, stars and mother and
father figures have been incorporated into Christian
festivals in Britain.

The area suffers extremes of climate, having
long, very cold winters and warm, but short sum-
mers. It was traditional for the men to carve wood
and the women to embroider, sitting round the stove
in the long, dark winter days. Like all northern Euro-
peans, they told us traditional stories or sagas, thus
preserving the old myths and legends handed down

(above) *This nineteenth-century embroidery is probably of peasant origin, worked in the north-west of the former USSR. It is worked on an evenweave linen fabric with linen embroidery threads in soft terracotta red with highlights of scarlet, orange, green, blue and black*
EG no 4492; 35 x 107cm (14³/4 x 42in)
(PHOTOGRAPHY: DUDLEY MOSS)

(left) *Detail of the embroidery* (PHOTOGRAPHY: DUDLEY MOSS)

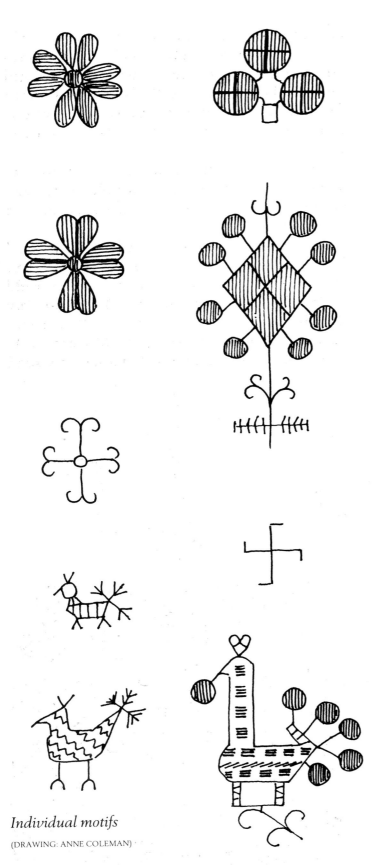

Individual motifs

(DRAWING: ANNE COLEMAN)

through generations. During the twelfth and thirteenth centuries, these ancient stories were recorded and depicted in manuscripts which were then probably used as source material for embroidery design.

The embroidery done by the Russian peasant women followed local tradition so exactly that it is possible to pin-point not only the region but the exact village where pieces were worked. Patterns and designs were passed down from one generation to the next and used as a means of identification as well as decoration. Whether the women knew or cared about the symbolism of their designs is not clear.

During most of the last thousand years, Russian peasants have lived social and cultural lives completely separate from the ruling classes. Even the Tartar invasions during the eleventh to thirteenth centuries which had such influence on the rest of Russia, hardly permeated this particular region where the peasants were often nomadic, living by hunting, fishing and trapping in the vast forests of fir and birch.

Embroidery was used to decorate costumes as well as household textiles. Embroidered towels were particularly important as religious accessories, and were used to decorate the corner of the room where the icon was kept. An icon is a sacred image or picture of Christ, or the Virgin, or a saint, and is a venerated item in the Russian Orthodox church. Towels were also used for important family and religious occasions, for example to decorate a wedding sleigh. Until quite recently, maybe even still, embroidered towels were hung on solitary birch trees, or on a wooden cross in the open air – a custom which is perhaps a relic from the days when the spirit of the tree had to be pacified with a gift. In general, Russian embroideries of this type are composed of a central figure, with less important figures and motifs on either side, and one side of the design mirrors the other. The designs are stylised. There is no perspective, and all the motifs, which are not to scale, are arranged in a pattern over the whole surface of the fabric.

The forward-facing figures, holding their hands high, are usually assumed to be earth gods, spirits of fecundity. Smaller human figures also face forwards, but animals are depicted in profile. The individual figures are also symmetrical, one side an exact mirror image of the other. It is interesting to speculate on these mirror image designs, and the fact that embroidered towels were also used to decorate mirrors; in many parts of the world, mirrors are thought to turn away the evil eye.

In this particular embroidery the most important, highly decorated figure, probably a mother goddess, is on the left (see colour plate on pages 98-9). The fabric has been cut next to this figure, so it seems likely that the original piece was cut in two. The goddess is flanked by a small figure in a sleigh or a boat, with double-headed animals, and trees with birds, then another large figure. These last two arrangements are repeated.

Right across the base of the work is a zig-zag bor-der, thought to represent water. Flowers and birds, devices like swastikas, and also circles which are generally accepted as symbols for the sun, are arranged on the background. One particular sun motif is often found on embroidery connected with wedding garments, as it also symbolises the start of life in a new home.

All but the smallest motifs are decorated with vertical linear patterns based on simple straight, zig-zag and curved lines to give a very rich and exuberant all-over pattern.

The basic fabric is evenweave linen. This would have been a cheap material at the time, as Russia was one of the biggest producers of flax in the world during the nineteenth century. The embroidery threads are also linen, in a soft terracotta red with highlights of scarlet, orange, green, blue and black. Red was considered not only to be the most beautiful

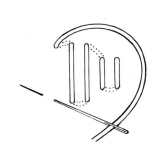
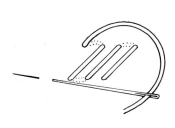
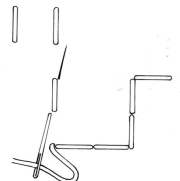

Motif and linear patterns and diagrams of surface satin stitch and double running stitch
(DRAWING: ANNE COLEMAN)

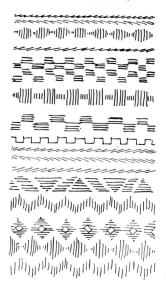
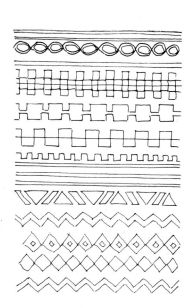

CHAPTER SEVENTEEN

FABULOUS BEASTS

Daphne Nicholson

THE EMBROIDERY illustrated appears to be part of a longer border, super-frontal or runner, probably worked in the seventeenth century. It measures 21 x 66cm (8¼ x 26in). A running design of pairs of beasts, possibly unicorns or heavier horned animals with separated manes, are depicted facing each other and drinking at fountains – which perhaps symbolise the fountain of life. They are separated by stylised trees, birds and huntsmen blowing horns and leading hounds.

The motifs are voided, only the background being worked, but the shapes are outlined with double running or Holbein stitch, and the beasts are decorated with small spot designs and a few lines to emphasise form and clarify details of eyes, manes and so on. On the fountains, water gushes from lions' mouths into wide bowls supported by tree forms. At the top and bottom of this fragment is a border with a repeat design of a small plant motif. The background between the motifs is worked in two-sided Italian cross stitch.

The embroidery is similar to the technique called Assisi-work which, since the beginning of the twentieth century, has been associated with the town and district of Assisi in northern Italy. It is now a domestic industry in that area and an important source of income through tourism. The technique and designs developed from local embroideries of the thirteenth and fourteenth centuries, which accounts for the primitive and mythical form of many of the birds and animals. This example is worked in two-sided Italian cross stitch, but similar embroideries have backgrounds worked in long-legged cross stitch and eyelets. In this example evenweave linen of 38 threads to the inch/2.5cm was used. The two-sided Italian cross stitch was worked in red thread, and with a blunt needle to ensure that the background threads were not split.

Assisi embroidery is worked on a counted thread linen, using a silk or perlé thread of a suitable thickness. The design is usually transferred by the traditional method of tracing and tacking through the lines of the drawing onto the linen. Alternatively, a photocopy of the design can be painted with a solution of water, white spirit and detergent and ironed to the background fabric.

The motifs are outlined in double running or Holbein stitch, and the background is worked in one of the following stitches: cross stitch, long-legged cross stitch, two-sided Italian cross stitch or eyelets. The fountains, birds and huntsmen in the embroidery are similar to those seen in early medieval illuminated manuscripts and tiles, and also in the Mappa Mundi in Hereford Cathedral – this is a twelfth-century map of the world, depicting many fantastic animals. Similar motifs are seen in other embroideries from the sixteenth and seventeenth centuries.

The unicorn featured in the fragment illustrated is a popular motif which occurs in many textiles, including the early sixteenth-century set of French tapestries known as 'La Dame à la Licorne', and the late fifteenth-century tapestry of the legend of St Stephen, both of which can be seen in the Cluny Museum in Paris. It was introduced to England at the time of the union of England and Scotland in 1602, but had been used in Scotland since the time of James I (of Scotland) in 1406. Scottish gold coins, struck during the reign of James III, were called 'unicorns' because the unicorn is shown on one side of the coin, carrying the royal arms. The unicorn is now a supporter of the British royal arms. In *The Queen's Beasts* by H. Stanford (1953), the unicorn is described as being a white or cream-coloured beast with horn, hoofs, mane, beard and tail-tuft in gold, wearing a gold collar and chain. One possible origin of the unicorn may be in the pre-Christian bas-reliefs of the bulls of Ninevah which show only one horn because they are always depicted from the side.

Fabulous beasts come from dreams or myths from the mists of time, and can still be found in modern folklore. Many people believe in the Yeti, said to be living in the Himalayas, and in Big Foot of the Canadian Rockies. For my purposes, after studying different types of beasts from various sources including prehistoric paintings, heraldry, early textiles, childrens' books and the myths and legends of many lands, it seemed appropriate to conjure up a new beast from the imagination.

Before embarking on more experimental work, I stitched a small embroidery in traditional Assisi-

Fabulous beasts from various sources; Lascaux, the Book of Kells and the Mappa Mundi

(DRAWING: DAPHNE NICHOLSON)

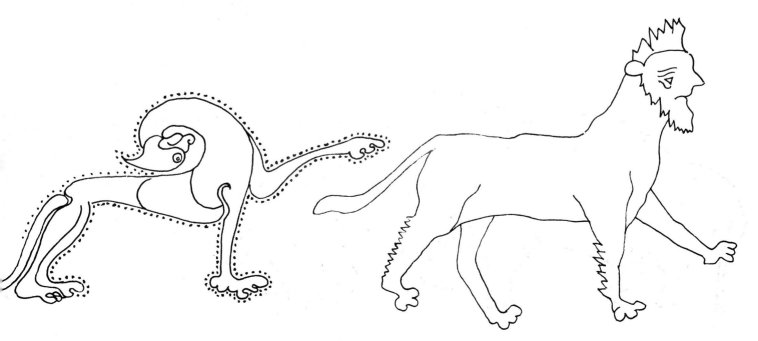

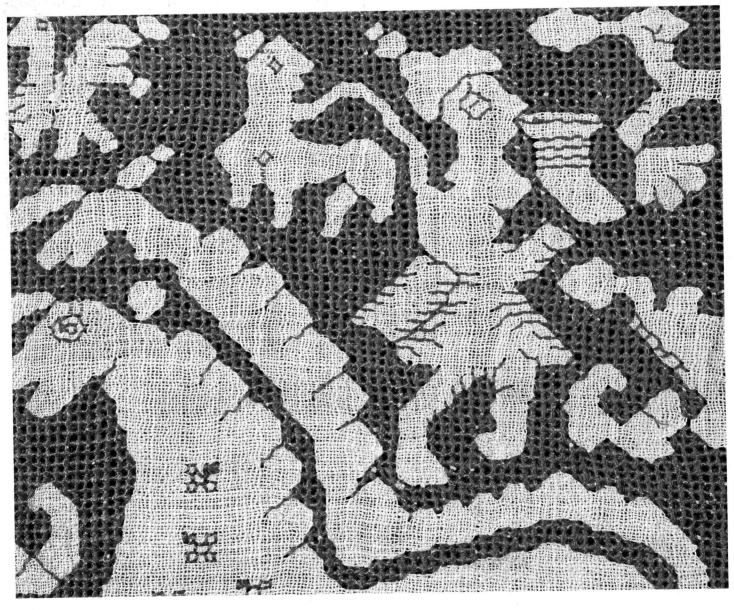

(above left) *Assisi embroidery showing a design of pairs of beasts, possibly unicorns or heavier horned animals with separated manes. The motifs are outlined with double running or Holbein stitch, and the background between the motifs is worked in two-sided Italian cross stitch*
EG no 1966; 21 x 6cm (8 1/4 x 26in)

(PHOTOGRAPHY: DUDLEY MOSS)

(above) *Modern interpretation of Assisi-work. Strips of white linen and ribbons were applied to a background fabric. Stitches include long-legged cross. Designed and worked by Daphne Nicholson* (PHOTOGRAPHY: PETER READ)

(left) *Detail of embroidery showing a stylised figure*

(PHOTOGRAPHY: DUDLEY MOSS)

a) Holbein stitch

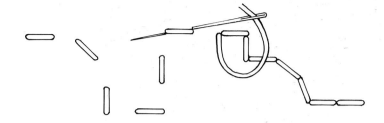

b) Algerian eye stitch

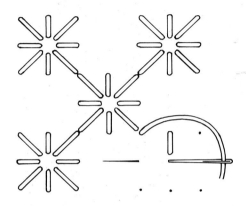

c) Cross stitch

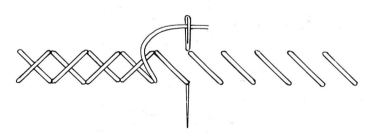

d) Two-sided Italian cross stitch

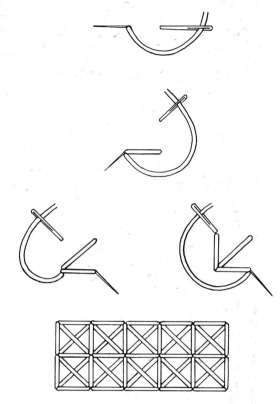

e) Long-legged cross stitch
(DRAWING: MOLLIE PICKEN)

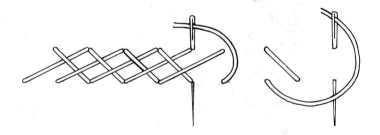

work using the unicorn from 'La Dame à la Licorne' as the design. The animal was outlined in Holbein stitch, and cross stitch was used to cover the background.

An imaginary beast was drawn and several photocopies taken, which were cut up and re-arranged in different ways. This method produces accidental design together with an atmosphere of mystery and extravagance. A photocopy of the

Traditional Assisi-work using cross stitch. Unicorn from 'La Dame à la Licorne'. Designed and worked by Daphne Nicholson (PHOTOGRAPHY: PETER READ)

chosen design was cut into strips and transferred to white linen, leaving 2.5cm (1in) of fabric between each strip. To maintain the Assisi-work theme the motif was voided and the background of each strip worked in long-legged cross stitch. The embroidered strips were cut out and applied to a background fabric with ribbons sewn between them, covering the cut edges. Finally the ribbons were stitched over with a white thread to co-ordinate the design and give an effect of counter-change.

A simpler horizontal design could have been worked, but this would have lacked the effective movement of the final solution.

CHAPTER EIGHTEEN

CZECH GEOMETRY INTO COMPUTER GRIDS

Valerie Campbell-Harding

THE CHILD'S BONNET illustrated is labelled as coming from Hungary, but research has found that it is more likely to have been made in Czechoslovakia. However, flexible boundaries between European countries mean that it is very difficult to pinpoint the country.

The Czechs and the Hungarians are both embroidery-loving peoples. Embroidery is worn by both men and women, and is used in the house on articles such as pillow-cases, tablecloths, bonnets, coifs, aprons, men's shorts and women's shifts. Often the embroidery was worked as borders on strips of linen, and joined to the main fabric with insertion stitches, a convenient way of working. Sometimes lace was an added decoration, as on this bonnet. These embroideries were worked by peasant women for their own use and that of their families, and also by groups of women in manor houses. Geometric patterns are characteristic, although the motifs are not exclusively from Czechoslovakia or Hungary and can also be found in neighbouring countries.

Satin stitch, both counted and freely worked, is often used, as on this bonnet. There is a little added chain stitch (worked using a needle, with 20 stitches per inch/2.5cm) giving finer lines of colour in some places. The embroidery is worked on a linen with 42 threads per inch, and as the stitches are very regular, it must have been counted. The embroidery on the piece at the back of the head is 15cm (6in) deep and 15cm (6in) wide, gathered at the top to give the rounded shape; and the embroidered strip over the head is 5cm (2in) deep and 28cm (11in) wide, joined to the back piece with an unusual insertion stitch. The front edge is of tape lace.

The appeal of this bonnet is the richness of the solidly worked stitching, contrasted with the plain areas, and the combination of many different shapes and patterns in the one small article. The colours are delightful, with an interesting tonal variation given by the changes in direction of the stitchery. It is still as bright on the right side as on the wrong, an indication that for most of the time the bonnet was kept hidden away.

One of the elements chosen to include in the designs, and the embroidery based on them, was the idea of strips or borders made separately and joined afterwards, either to each other or onto a background. Other ideas included combining different motifs in the borders, and recreating the richness of stitchery seen in the original.

For the colour scheme it seemed right to keep the colours seen in the bonnet: blue, orange, bright yellow, orange/yellow and grey/green, but using black instead of ivory for depth of tone, and gold for extra richness. Rust was added (black added to the orange), and yellow ochre, to give more warmth to the scheme, even though they were not in the original.

In order to avoid merely copying original embroideries, it is helpful to move into different design methods and techniques. In this case different drawing and paint programmes were used on the

Child's bonnet, probably from Czechoslovakia, although labelled as Hungarian. The background fabric is linen, and the embroidery is worked mainly in satin stitch. The front edge is of tape lace
EG no 2385; 23 x 42cm (9 x 16½in)

(PHOTOGRAPHY: DUDLEY MOSS)

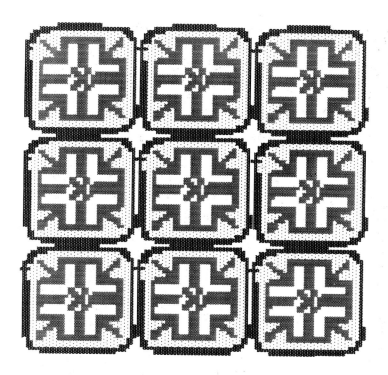

The shapes drawn on the computer and (right) repeated to make borders

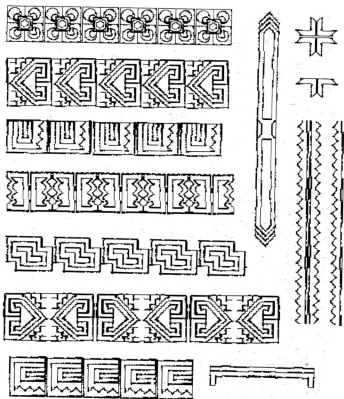

computer, and individual shapes were drawn from the original patterns on the screen, then multiplied, building up many different border patterns in black and white to obtain the correct shapes, sizes and combinations. Using a 'stretch' facility, which pulls elements on the screen, it was easy to make the borders the same length and to fit the proportions of the book cover. This would be used to hold a thick stack of A4 sheets of paper showing the design variations found in the bonnet, as well as the sample.

The patterns were coloured in using the 'bucket fill' facility within the black line drawings. This gave a stained-glass-window look to the designs which was a useful starting-point, and suggested black edges to the individual shapes. Different colour combinations were tried, with and without the black lines. Extra colours and textures were added, using different computer tools and effects to arrive at designs that suggested stitchery. One of the great advantages of computer designing is the ability to 'try something and see' very quickly, and to provide alternative lay-

Computer design of the borders made to fit the proportions of the book cover

outs and colour schemes from which to choose. Having this choice is an essential part of the design process: so often one stops at the first idea, instead of pushing the possibilities further and having the freedom to select the best design among many.

Although it was decided to make a book with an embroidered cover, another possibility would have been to adapt the designs for decoration on dress or household objects such as sheets, towels or pillowcases. Small bags and mirror frames are also able to carry the sort of rich texture and embroidery which were built up in layers for the book cover.

The next stage was the working of the stitched samples, so that a choice could be made for the final piece. Machine embroidery would give the essential shift away from copying the hand-stitchery of the original, and yet include the same richness and fine detail. Various stitches and thread combinations were tried on different fabrics: I chose those which gave the right colour mix and density of stitching, the right texture and general 'look' and, even more important, the bulk and handle that was wanted for the finished piece.

Strips of painted silk and painted satin ribbons

(left) *Book cover in machine embroidery, using a variety of machine-embroidery threads including metallics. Painted and dyed fabrics were used, together with small areas of gold leaf. Designed and worked by Valerie Campbell-Harding* (PHOTOGRAPHY: PETER READ)

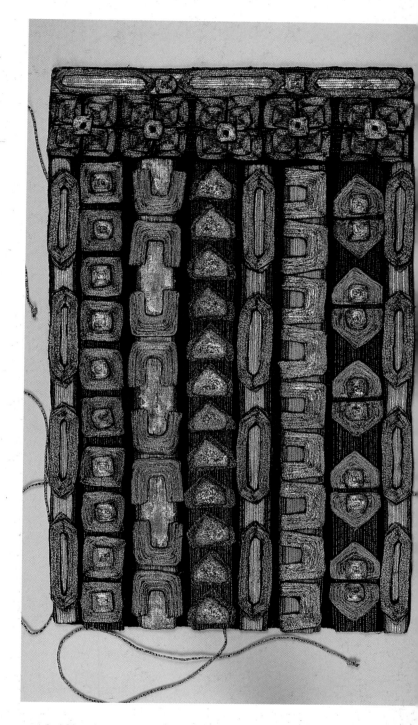

Back of book cover. Designed and worked by Valerie Campbell-Harding (PHOTOGRAPHY: PETER READ)

were bonded onto black cotton, which itself was bonded to black felt. Long strips of this were cut out and covered with lines of straight machine-stitching, using black thread on the bobbin and a colour plus a variegated gold thread through the needle. The coloured thread was changed frequently during working, but the gold thread remained throughout. Couched gold cord was added to some of the samples.

Finally the embroidery was worked as separate pieces, some on black muslin, but most of them on a sandwich of black cotton bonded to felt. Free machine running and whip stitch were used, again with two threads through the needle – a colour and the variegated thread, and at different tensions. Black thread in the bobbin affected the colour when the top tension was tightened so that some pieces were darker than others. The pieces worked on the muslin were completely covered with granite stitch to give a change of texture. When the small pieces were embroidered they were cut out of the sandwich and the edges burnt to neaten them and darken the colour. Gold leaf was added on top of the stitching on some pieces and then more stitching worked over it to knock it back as it was rather bright and shiny.

When enough pieces had been prepared, they were laid on the embroidered strips to form the borders, usually two (sometimes three) layers deep, and stitched lightly to hold them in place. A backing for the book cover was made of black felt with black cotton bonded to both sides, which was closely quilted with black thread to give a firm base. The strips were laid in place and finally stitched down.

Four cords were stitched to the inside of the book cover to hold the pages in place, and another thicker cord was made by zig-zagging over macramé cord to wrap round the whole book.

CHAPTER NINETEEN

SCULPTURED GOLD

Chris Berry

THROUGHOUT HISTORY, conspicuous elaborate decoration on costume and furnishing, both secular and ecclesiastical, has implied wealth and status. The intrinsic value inherent in gold and silver threads, together with the beautiful light-catching effects of raised metal-thread embroidery has challenged professional and amateur embroiderers to develop great skill in this technique. As early as the fifteenth century, countries such as Spain, Germany and Hungary were producing altar frontals and ecclesiastical vestments in high relief metal-thread embroidery. It was also used for the trappings of ceremonial and heraldic work, vestments, costume, uniforms and purses for the Great Seal. By the eighteenth century, this technique flourished throughout Europe.

The embroideries illustrated are three eighteenth-century Spanish fragments in metal-thread embroidery, and an unidentified fragment. The Spanish pieces show metal-thread work in low relief worked directly on the background, a technique known in the eighteenth century as 'guipure' or 'guimped' embroidery. They are exquisitely embroidered, particularly the vine motif with its gold-covered padded leaf and grapes of domed metal shapes. The vine leaf has a foundation of card stained yellow to match the metal thread. Sometimes vellum, stained with saffron, was used for this purpose. Silver-gilt passing thread is laid back and forth across the shape, held at each change of direction by a small stitch. This thread is a flat metal strip (battu) over a yellow silk, slightly twisted when worked, producing a sparkling, glinting appearance. The veins of the leaf are small paillettes (sequins) held in place with bouillon (a metal coil of rounded gold wire) cut into small pieces and threaded onto the holding stitches.

The grapes are made from coloured spangles cut from thin sheets of silver varnished in different colours, and attached to the fabric by four pieces of bouillon. The spaces between are filled with smaller pieces of cut purl, and two thicknesses of gold-covered twisted silk cord form the stem of the motif, the thinner inner cord being couched in double lines in brick stitch.

The triangular leaves consist of a rounded silver-gilt passing thread couched with beige silk in a chevron pattern, and the flower petals are worked in basket stitch, using plate over couched string. A small undeveloped leaf is guipe work, also using plate. The outlines are in gold-covered twisted silk thread, known in the eighteenth century as Milanese braid, which is made of two silk cords twisted in opposite directions, wound together and covered with battu (flattened gold wire).

The larger unidentified fragment is worked in high relief, a technique called 'Rapport' embroidery. The individually embroidered motifs are cut out, applied and usually outlined with cord or Milanese braid. The working of this fragment is similar to many examples found in western Europe, particularly France, during the eighteenth century and is possibly part of court dress. The design shows two intertwining stems with leaves, buds and flowers of different plants. Heavy card padding, varying in thickness, is stained yellow and in some places has cracked with use. These card shapes could have been glued or basted into place. All the embroidery except for one domed paillon was previously worked on a backing of white ribbed silk, cut out and applied to the background. So as not to tarnish the gold

Ideas for jewellery superimposed on the piece from the Embroiderers' Guild Collection (PHOTOGRAPHY: JIM PASCOE)

(above) *Eighteenth-century fragments from Spain. On a background of silk woven with silver strips, in silver-gilt passing thread, rough purl, plate and spangles are embroidered floral motifs: vine leaf and grapes 7 x 5.7cm (2³/4 x 2¹/4in); flower and leaf 7 x 6cm (2³/4 x 2³/8in); leaf 4 x 2.3cm (1¹/2 x 1in) EG no 1182; eighteenth century*
(PHOTOGRAPHY: DUDLEY MOSS)

(right) *Eighteenth-century unidentified fragment, probably from western Europe: on a background of ribbed silk backed with linen, applied highly raised metal-thread motifs are embroidered in silver-gilt passing thread, rough purl, paillettes (sequins) and paillons. 48 x 11cm (19 x 4¹/4in)*
(PHOTOGRAPHY: DUDLEY MOSS)

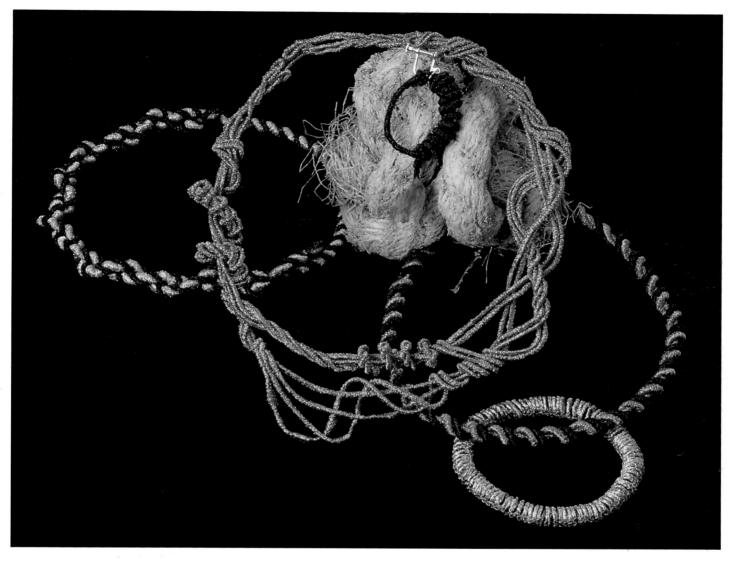

thread while it was being worked, it was wound on to a spindle, and only the spindle was handled.

The beauty of metal-thread work depends on the play of light on the surfaces of the threads, and it is important to use a variety of threads. Two types of passing thread (a round smooth and a flat wavy) are used, together with rough purl, couched Milanese braid, paillettes and paillon. The highly raised padded areas are worked as the vein leaf in the Spanish fragments but using double threads instead of single, in either smooth or slightly twisted passing threads. Slits and depressions in these raised areas are emphasised (and the holding stitches hidden) with a purple silk cord or Milanese braid.

It is fascinating to see the different effects produced by the same thread. For example the rough purl is used as a padding of threads for stems and

A display of neckpieces based on the versatile coiling construction. The main piece is based on a drawing of twisted tree-roots and vines. Designed and worked by Chris Berry (PHOTOGRAPHY: JIM PASCOE)

small branches, and over card padding for the base of a flower bud. Other effects are produced by using loops of cut purl in various ways.

The only part of this embroidery to be worked directly on the background fabric is a domed paillon which is encircled with check purl held through four points. This type of purl, known as 'frisure' in eighteenth-century France, was made from flattened wire wound round a square bar. During the thirteenth century, silver drawn wire was gilded and flattened into a 'lamella' which was then wrapped around a silk core.

CHAPTER TWENTY

PERSIAN POMEGRANATES

Jenny Blackburn

ALTHOUGH THE label on these items illustrated designates them as being from Kashmir, the card index of the Guild Collection has had the word 'Kashmir' deleted and 'Persian' substituted. Comparative study of three Persian runners, also in the Guild Collection (Nos 3359, 2321 and 4004) shows such a similarity in design and techniques that the items here can almost certainly be assumed Persian, and stitched with a needle rather than being tamboured.

The late nineteenth-century bag and purse, measuring 13.5 x 20cm (5¼ x 7¾in) and 7 x 10cm (2¾ x 4in) respectively, are solidly worked in silk thread on a fine linen background, which is visible in some areas. They are both lined with purple silk and neatened with a self-coloured bias binding made from the purple silk. The design consists of repeating motifs of stylised pomegranates with a repeating border pattern of carnations, and is worked in chain stitch, stem stitch, and couched thread. As the design runs in different directions on each piece it can be assumed that these items were made from one piece of fabric, probably at a later date. The cutting up and recycling of textiles from this region was not uncommon during the nineteenth century, when the work became popular in the West. Small changes of colour, the areas worked in slightly thicker thread in green and mauve, occur mainly on the border edge of each piece, which could indicate that whoever made this piece of textile into these items tried to repair what would have been a worn edge of the original.

The bias-edged strip, used as a stay for the bag flap, is also cut from the original textile and has been sewn into place with the design slightly offset. Whether this was accidental or deliberate is a matter for conjecture, but it is somehow in keeping with the other irregular features of the work; for example, the colour change in one motif on the purse where a darker red thread is suddenly introduced is probably original, whereas the other changes in the thread colour are possibly repairs as previously mentioned.

The main irregularity lies, however, in the design itself. Across most of the fabric the repeating pomegranate motifs and triangular designs in the intervening spaces run in regular lines. However, on the bag flap next to the border, the stylised pomegranates change from an elegant wine glass shape to a bulbous, distorted, swollen heart. As there appears to be no reason for this distortion of the simple repeat pattern we can only assume that it is deliberate, and can perhaps be attributed to the Islamic concept that nothing is perfect save Allah.

Each pomegranate motif is worked predominantly in red with one row of yellow chain stitch, and outlined with black stem stitch. The top of each motif has a line of buff-coloured silk couched with black. Further outlines and part of the intervening space between the pomegranates are worked in green chain stitch, with the other spaces filled with red chain stitch. The inner edge of the border pattern also uses chain stitch, worked diagonally in alternating dark green and yellow. The carnations of the border pattern are worked solely in chain stitch in a dark blue/green with a red outline and centre. It is

Bag and purse in silk thread on a fine linen background. The design consists of repeating motifs of stylised pomegranates with a border pattern of carnations EG no 341; late nineteenth century; Kashmir; bag 13.5 x 20cm (5¼ x 7¾in); purse 7 x 10cm (2¾ x 4in); given by Mrs Turner-Wood, 1961
(PHOTOGRAPHY: DUDLEY MOSS)

mainly in this area that repairs seem to have been carried out, in pale green and mauve thread.

The fruit and flowers of the pomegranate appear frequently in Middle Eastern art, especially in embroidery. One of the earliest references we have to its use in embroidery is to be found in the Bible, in Exodus 28 vv 29–33: 'And beneath the hem of it thou shalt make pomegranates of blue and of purple and of scarlet, round about the hem thereof; and bells of gold between them round about'.

Because of the large number of seeds it produces, the pomegranate has long been regarded as a symbol of fertility, and the colour red is also symbolic. The other flower represented is the carnation, also a symbol of pure love and fertility. Both the pomegranate and carnation are used repeatedly in embroideries of the Middle East, and countries which bordered Persia (now Iran) assimilated Persian influences in their design. This cross fertilisation of design ideas was facilitated by the fact that Persia was on the Silk Route from East to West, and the designs of Persia spread to both East and West, reaching England at the end of the fifteenth century.

After initial study of the piece was complete, the first process was to consider ways forward. The irregularity of the design pattern was particularly interesting, and the fact that the piece was worked in solid stitching tied in with my own work at the time, which was exploring how solid machine-stitching can mould and shape fabric. Although the original embroidery is completely flat, perhaps the shapes when worked in solid machining would cause the fabric to distort.

The use of narrow bias binding as a finish was considered, as bias strips could be used to provide 'full stops' or as grid structures. The changes of colour within the embroidery were interesting and could be adapted into the contemporary work. Various ideas were set out on paper, and the next stage was to decide which ones to pursue and how to set about developing them.

A pomegranate shape was cut into a potato and printed onto sheets of paper. Experiments were made using regular, repeat patterns, borders and circular motifs, in one colour as well as overprinting with a second colour, thus producing interesting mixes of colour and changing the spaces between the motif. Unfortunately none of the sheets produced anything which inspired me on that particular day! Using potato prints does, however, provide a lot of ideas relatively quickly.

Still thinking of printing as the design method and wishing to pursue the theme of the irregular shape on the purse, a string printing block was made, by sticking medium-thick parcel string to a cardboard square with PVA glue. When the glue was thoroughly dry, rubbings were taken using wax crayons, and the resultant sheets painted over. Using ready-mix paint on paper, the string block produced the most satisfactory results. Wishing now to get on with the stitchery, two main ideas were begun.

Stitching the pomegranate shape with metal thread on the machine, closely following the contours of the shape, produced a very raised piece of stitchery. In keeping with the regular repeat pattern of the original pieces, a design was made in cut paper. Thinking of Persian miniatures, I decided to keep the piece small, with solid regular stitching making a framework for a very free centre. The centre was to be very rich, and took its inspiration from the back of the Persian runner originally studied alongside the purse. Layers of rich gold fabrics were machined together and slashed with a knife, thus giving a distressed appearance to the textile. Further 'ends of threads' were added in the form of the tufts made from machine-embroidery threads. This centre piece was inserted behind the framework of raised pomegranate shapes.

Wishing to continue working on the theme but also to explore other aspects of the work, the same irregular-shaped motif was used again. A recurring idea was that of fragments, and this project seemed to be an ideal opportunity to use some of the precious pieces of fabrics I had collected over many years. These pieces were assembled on a calico backing, often using the reverse or a faded part of the material to give the desired effect. Fabric paints were used to blend the colours. The pieces were stitched into place using straight-stitch free machine embroidery. The next step was to incorporate the design element, and my original string block was used to print onto the fabric with coloured and metallic fabric paint.

a)

a) *Carnation and pomegranate from a Persian carpet*
b) *Nineteenth-century Middle Eastern motif in metal thread with chain stitch*
c) *Various pomegranate motifs*
(DRAWINGS: JENNY BLACKBURN)

b)

c)

The finished piece, inspired by Persian miniatures, with regular stitching making a framework for a very free centre. Designed and worked by Jenny Blackburn
(PHOTOGRAPHY: STUART BARKER)

(left) *Detail of modern development using a collection of fabrics machine-stitched onto a calico backing and over-printed with coloured and metallic fabric paint. Designed and worked by Jenny Blackburn*
(PHOTOGRAPHY: STUART BARKER)

Although intended to be a machine-embroidered panel, I considered it important to retain the chain stitch as on the original embroidery. This was achieved by using a Singer 700/720 Touch and Sew machine which produces a chain stitch. Areas of the textile were solidly worked with machine chain stitch, while the design shapes were emphasised with free machining in coloured and metallic thread in straight stitch and narrow satin stitch.

The finished textile was mounted on a pure wool dark maroon background, retaining the irregular edge of the fragmented piece. Of the two pieces I think this was the most successful as a resolved piece of work.

CHAPTER TWENTY-ONE

THREE FRAGMENTS FROM THE MIDDLE EAST

Jean Mould

INITIAL RESEARCH into the origins of the fragments illustrated suggested many influences. From the fifteenth to the nineteenth centuries numerous military conflicts involving eastern countries such as Greece, Turkey and India, together with the opening up of trade and travel with the West, resulted in the import as well as export of new materials and ideas. Persian carpets and rugs showed a powerful use of pattern, emphasising the abstraction of plants and flowers into geometric shapes, producing rich borders and repeat units; these must have influenced the British embroiderer who, in turn, sent pattern books from Britain for the Eastern embroiderer to copy, resulting in further exchanges of ideas.

Worked in tent stitch on a cotton background using a twisted silk thread, these densely stitched, multi-coloured fragments use stylised flowers as the design source. The soft pinks, blues and beiges used in England occur in one of the samples and although more formal in design, it bears a strong affinity with a piece of seventeenth-century English Turkey work in the Victoria and Albert Museum. The diagonal patterns would seem to be peculiar to the Reza region of Persia; they do not suggest a copying of design from a carpet or illuminated manuscript, as was usual. They have a more naturalistic look to them which may indicate that they were worked from English pattern books, or at least influenced by them from another source.

Each sample has a different quality. The small square is exquisitely worked on a finer ground fabric, and the stitches – unlike the other two examples – all lie in the same direction, perhaps indicating a more professional execution. Although miniature, the pattern is well defined and subtly organised. At first glance it would appear to be a repeating motif around four sides of a square, but in fact the fourth corner of the unit ends in a vase or root motif, suggesting a right way up.

The other two fragments are more coarsely stitched, with the design varying in stylisation; but a seemingly overall pattern has the main motifs ending in stems, leaves and roots. All three have edges showing unpicked seams. This type of embroidery was very popular throughout Europe in the nineteenth century, and larger samples were often cut up to produce cushions, bags and garment pieces. One of these fragments could, in fact, be from a Persian trouser garment.

In those examples which bear a resemblance to English work, the pattern tends to come and go in definition. This could be due to wear, either the rubbing of the surface threads through use, or because it has been worked from the pattern books from England. These were not always clear and sufficiently well defined for someone unfamiliar with the particular motifs illustrated.

Without further research, many uncertainties hang over these embroideries. However, this does

Fragments of Middle Eastern embroideries, worked in tent stitch on a cotton background using a silk twist thread. These densely stitched, multi-coloured fragments use flowers as the design source in varying degrees of stylisation
EG no 2350; 27 x 20cm (10³/4 x 8in)
EG no 3627; 12 x 34cm (4³/4 x 13¹/2in)
Un-numbered; 15 x 14cm (6 x 5¹/2in)
(PHOTOGRAPHY: DUDLEY MOSS)

Basic equipment: *alternative screens; garden wires, plastic and rug canvases, nets and scrims*
Pulp sources: *wood shavings, computer paper, dried leaves and grasses, and cotton linters*
(PHOTOGRAPHY: JEAN MOULD)

not detract from their exquisite beauty, their richness, subtlety of design and colouring. Their undefined and obscure origins make them constantly intriguing and, having themselves been inspired by other sources, they continue to offer a wealth of design material for today's embroiderer.

As well as the qualities already mentioned of pattern and colour, the appeal of these pieces has much to do with the fact that they are small fragments which can be held, turned over, and rearranged; that they are samples, remnants, off-cuts – incomplete, worn, faded and frayed. In a similar way a sketchbook holds the attention: the spontaneity in the movement of line, shape and colour in trial pieces exploring an idea, gives an unsettled feel to the arrangement, and continually keeps the eye

moving. The finished work can so often lose this aspect and become static and dull.

Taking these qualities as inspiration, rather than any specific imagery or technique, and by emphasising some of them, two pieces of work evolved. One is in fact an assortment of samples displayed together; the other is a planned arrangement worked almost as one piece of paper in an attempt to produce a finished whole, while retaining the original fascination of a collection of samples randomly laid together.

Paper can be made from a cotton-fibre pulp to which other threads are added at the sheet-forming stage, a technique which creates a background fabric compatible with hand- and machine- embroidery. I personally choose hand made paper for my work because it is so versatile, and use it both as a material in its own right and sometimes in association with fabrics.

The basic material for making paper can be paper itself, for instance recycled envelopes, computer paper, wrapping papers, packaging and so on. Cot-

Lacy and frayed effects achieved with paper formed on meshes, and threads with edges torn or burned, and surfaces block printed (PHOTOGRAPHY: JEAN MOULD)

ton rags and plant fibres make beautiful papers, but take a great deal of soaking, beating and boiling in soda to break down ready for pulping. However, cotton can be purchased in sheet form, or linters, ready processed for pulping in a domestic blender.

A simple mould and deckle, drying cloths and a bowl are the only other items needed to produce a sheet of paper in the traditional manner. In most of these experiments however, the deckle – which forms the pulp into a sheet with straight edges – has been discarded to allow the pulp to spread across the mould so as to give a ragged edge to the newly formed sheet.

In some cases the mould is not used. The pulp is lifted from the bowl onto a cloth to which it will either adhere or be removed from when dry. This depends upon the quantity of synthetic fibres in the cloth: the more natural the fibres, the more the pulp will adhere. An open-weave fabric such as plumber's/plasterer's scrim, canvases, nets and wires will collect the pulp. Papers formed in this way can be pressed and dried as usual between cloths and boards, and, of course, lend themselves well to combining with fabric, threads and stitchery.

Aqueous dyes and a retention aid have been used, together with paints and inks, to colour the illustrated examples. A metallic powder and binding agent were used for the gold block prints. Coloured pulp can be made from coloured sugar or cartridge papers or coloured tissue, which tends to bleed and produces subtle, soft tones which can be very attractive indeed.

Apart from threads forming the basic structure of the contemporary work, surface stitchery has been used only to emphasise those aspects of the original I personally found intriguing. The piece is finished for me but could easily be taken as a stage in the development of an idea and be interpreted again in various embroidery techniques.

A piece worked as a whole, but suggesting that many separate samples have been assembled. Designed and worked by Jean Mould
(PHOTOGRAPHY: NIGEL FRANCIS)

CHAPTER TWENTY-TWO

PATTERNS FROM SYRIA

Jenny Bullen

ALTHOUGH DESCRIBED officially as 'a fragment', the illustrated item does in fact appear to be a finished piece of work as it is hemmed and embroidered around all sides. It is possibly an apron, although there are examples of Palestinian veils (in the Museum of Mankind) made in a similar shape. The whole piece measures 97 x 53cm (38 x 21in) and tapers to a point at one of the narrow ends.

Although Syria was an important textile weaving centre, this was mainly for the production of fine silk fabrics, and embroidery seems to have been relatively insignificant; and at present it is difficult to research at all into the stitched textiles of the area. Like the rest of the Levant, however, the region was greatly influenced by eastern European embroidery, especially Turkey and the Ottoman Empire. There is no information on the maker, date or exact provenance of the work shown here, although it has a distinct peasant feel to it. The fabric is a quite fine hand-woven linen and apart from one or two small frayed areas, it is still in good condition. No repairs or conservation work have been carried out.

The embroidery has been worked in silk threads in the following colours: dark navy blue; mid-blue; dark and pale pink; creamy yellow. Most of the threads appear to have been commercially dyed and this helps to date the work to the early nineteenth century. Shelagh Weir, in her book on Palestinian costume, states that aniline dyes were not introduced into the area until the beginning of this century, and were not in wide use until after World War I. An indigo-dyed thread has been used on the interlaced stitch in the border, though it has faded in several parts.

The predominant embroidery design is composed of an all-over repeat pattern of dark blue sprigs interspersed with tiny pink motifs. Sheila Paine (*Embroidered Textiles; Traditional Patterns from Five Continents*) says that the carnation was a popular motif for embroidery in Syria, often highly stylised into a hexagon shape, and it is quite possible that this is the basis for the motif in this particular piece of work. Most of the pattern has been worked in dark blue thread, although the embroiderer has worked some areas in a paler thread, apparently quite at random. There is no indication that the stitches were marked on the cloth before working, and it seems likely that they were counted by eye.

It was very difficult to identify the stitch used in the working of this motif. The thread is quite thick and the linen fabric very fine, which resulted in a very dense appearance. After inspection of the work under a powerful magnifying lens, the stitch appeared to be either back stitch or double running stitch. The actual pattern of stitches varies slightly from one motif to another, and it is apparent that the overall effect was more important to the embroiderer than the regularity of the stitchery. The centre of each motif is worked in diagonal satin stitch in yellow thread.

The border pattern is quite important, and is in a totally different style from the floral motif. The two long sides are finished with a narrow strip of interlaced insertion stitch worked in bands of colours, some of the thread indigo-dyed. At the pointed end the border is more elaborate. At the 'V' point is a band of embroidery consisting of rows of cross stitch worked in alternate colours. On either side of this are

A collage of assorted printed surfaces including fine wool challis, calico, evenweave linen and Japanese textured paper overlaid on a sheet of fine Indian handmade paper (PHOTOGRAPH: JIM PASCOE)

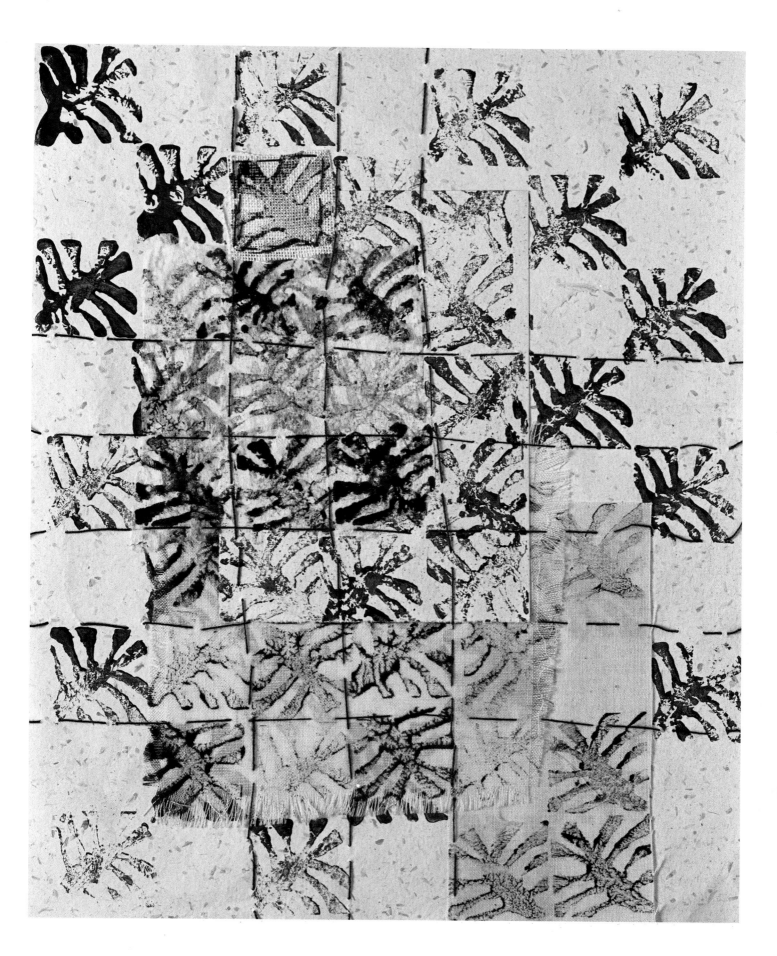

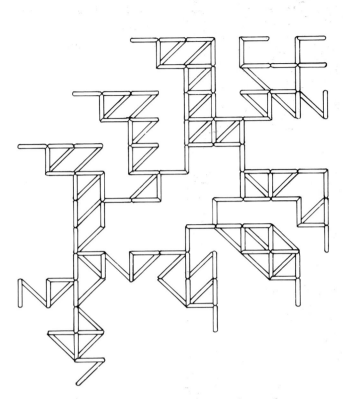

Stitches in the sprigged motif. The stitch used appears to be back stitch or double running worked on the straight and the diagonal of the fabric. It is impossible to state either where each motif begins and ends, or the direction taken of the stitches. They appear to have been worked entirely at the whim of the embroiderer
(DRAWING: MOLLIE PICKEN)

Here a natural-coloured fine evenweave linen was used as a background for an alternative repeat pattern sequence. Printed squares from a coarser-weight fabric have been applied to the ground fabric. Lines of running stitch have again been used to hold the fabrics in place
(PHOTOGRAPH: JIM PASCOE)

handmade straw paper which was eventually used as the base of a panel. The pattern was then printed on various evenweave fabrics which were chosen in an attempt to retain some of the feel of the original embroidery.

Stitchery was again a problem, as it seemed that any form of embellishment was an intrusion. However, this could probably be overcome with the addition of coloured threads, if not coloured fabric dyes. Eventually, a minimum of stitchery was decided upon, mainly straight stitches in a dark blue cotton thread, and various experimental pieces were stitched. Some of the fragments were stitched together to make a tiny book.

The finished results were a long way from the original, and one must wonder if the peasant woman in her remote Syrian village would ever recognise her work from these modern examples. A lot of problems remain unsolved in the contemporary work. As a print the work appears quite satisfactory, but perhaps wrong choices were made for the embroidery. The addition of colour would have brought liveliness to the work but would have posed more problems for the embroiderer, and some of the aesthetic quality of the design would have been lost. However, exciting results could be obtained by overprinting in metallic dyes or one other colour, such as dark red, and then using a matching thread for stitchery.

The pieces illustrated here are only the start of a study which could provide the embroiderer with work for many years to come!

Cover of book. Designed and worked by Jenny Bullen
(PHOTOGRAPH: JIM PASCOE)

NEEDLEWOVEN BORDER

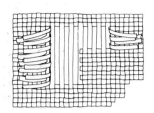
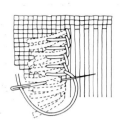

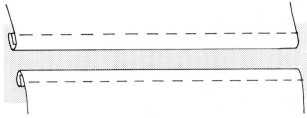

a) Withdraw threads from background fabric as shown to required depth and width. Turn back withdrawn threads and buttonhole in place. Carefully trim threads away

a) Joining pieces of fabric by means of an insertion stitch. Turn under narrow hems on facing edges and tack to strong paper (later removed), to give required space

b) Alternatively, turn back withdrawn threads and darn into fabric

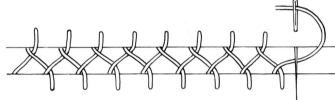

b) Simple insertion stitch

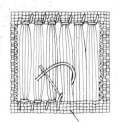
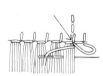

c) Remaining threads can be hemstitched into bundles if wished, but this is not obligatory

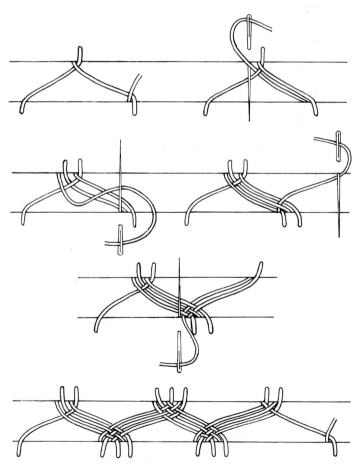

d) Simple needleweaving on remaining threads using a figure-of-eight movement. Start by running thread into fabric above starting-point so eventually it can be invisibly threaded into the weaving. Finish in the same way

e) Method of using two or more colours in a diagonal pattern   (DRAWINGS: MOLLIE PICKEN)

c) Plaited insertion stitch. A variation of this stitch includes a double knot at each intersection where the threads cross   (DRAWINGS: MOLLIE PICKEN)

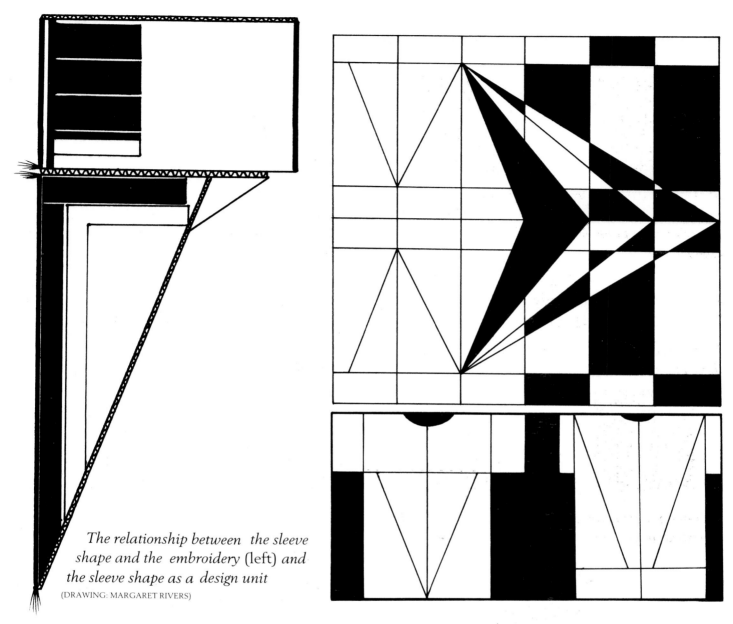

The relationship between the sleeve shape and the embroidery (left) *and the sleeve shape as a design unit*
(DRAWING: MARGARET RIVERS)

tinues on the upper and lower sections of the sleeve and, because one fabric is finer than the other, the lower part is smaller in scale. Apart from this border, there seems little relationship between the embroidery on the two parts of the sleeve. The style of the heavy, rich embroidery on the upper section is similar to that of some embroidery of Eastern Europe, notably Bulgaria. The Victoria & Albert Museum is unable to give an exact location and suggests the provenance 'East Mediterranean'.

The embroidery also includes double running stitch, eyelets, cross stitch, half cross stitch and a buttonholed edging. There is a small tassel at the lower point of the sleeve, and another on the forward edge of the front and back.

There are no clues as to the maker of the sleeve, but it was probably a woman (since embroidery is mainly a woman's occupation in this area) in Syria or the Northern Levant, either a member of a nomadic tribe subject to many outside influences, or a housewife in a settled community, thriftily and skilfully making a new dress from available materials.

The sleeve is an amalgam of influences and ideas, some of which became the inspiration for a small bag – a 'collector's piece' – the shape of which lends itself to an arrangement of borders. One edges the top of the bag, and the others surround the central panel, these emphasising the shape as they did on the sleeve. The Tree of Life motif is based on the one on the sleeve. It was tempting to use too many ideas as

CHAPTER TWENTY-FOUR

TURKISH MOSAIC IN COLOUR AND GOLD

Chris Berry

NARROW TOWELS like the one illustrated are sometimes referred to as sashes, and would have been used as items of costume as well as napkins. Turkish women at the baths would wrap their hair in a long towel, and wear a towel as a sash over their caftans, or thread one through the top of wide trousers.

Examples from the seventeenth century show the embroidery in two bands across the width of the towel, a major and a minor band. The gap gradually decreased until in the nineteenth century there is one band usually about 20cm (8in) deep, as seen here. In this design, however, it is possible to discern a major and a minor band: the minor band consists of a leaf and 'flower' motif linked by oblique stems, and the major band of a repeat motif of a geometrical bunch of grapes surrounded by a similar leaf and flower border. This towel is completely reversible; though finely worked, it contains some very obvious inaccuracies, such as the colour changing in mid-leaf as well as the stitch direction, together with the inconsistent use of various metal threads in the patterned areas.

In general these embroidered towels show a small variety of stitches, and this example is no exception. Because of the small scale of these stitches, executed in a slightly twisted silk, and combined with the fineness of the undyed cotton fabric, they are difficult to identify. Stitches commonly used in Turkish towels are double running, double darning, 'embroiderers' stitch' (satin stitch), and musabak stitch (a pulled stitch combining single and reverse faggot). A useful clue to the musabak stitch used for the leaves, is the colour change, which, being diagonal, indicates that the stitch must have been worked in that direction. The stems, grape grid and grape outline, and the outlines of the leaves and flowers, are all worked in a variety of double running stitches.

The attractive textured appearance is achieved by the use of gold plate alternating with passing thread, worked with four threads in one needle. Traditionally the plate was pushed through the fabric by hand, not with a needle. Here it lies flat, and the threads of the background fabric are undamaged, a difficult technique but very well executed in this piece.

Embroidered cloths variously named squares (Çevre), towels (peskir), and sashes (long towels) served a multiplicity of functions within the Turkish household. These embroidered towels were used all across the Middle East, although the word 'towel' should not be applied too literally. They were also used as wrappings for precious objects, for letters and as items of costume. Elaborately decorated towels were used at ritual ceremonial occasions, and it was the custom for a Turkish bride to be presented with a distinctively embroidered towel on her wedding day.

At meal times embroidered towels could be table linen, napkins or drying cloths. A letter written in 1718 by Lady Montagu describing a visit to the Sultana Hafiten states that the costly napkins, embroidered with silks and gold, were entirely spoiled before dinner was over. Two hundred years later a Mrs Ramsey, writing about everyday life in Turkey, notes that a narrow napkin 'many yards in length,

Modern experiment superimposed on the Turkish towel (PHOTOGRAPHY: JIM PASCOE)

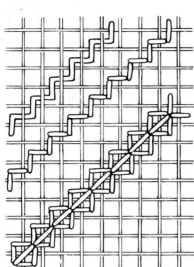

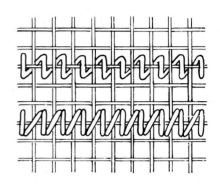

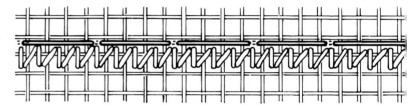

Double running stitch in steps on either side of a double running stitch on the diagonal

Double running stitch with dog-tooth edge. Below this it is shown edged with double running over four threads (seen in outline of grapes and smaller metal thread motifs) (DRAWINGS: MOLLIE PICKEN)

and with finely embroidered borders', lay in loose folds on the laps of the diners who were sitting around a circular metal tray, three feet (a metre) in diameter, placed on an upturned stool. The tablecloth 'of patchwork, like a quilt' was under the table on the floor.

It seems likely that from the seventeenth century onwards every Turkish household possessed a large collection of these ubiquitous 'towels'. Though traditionally worked in the seclusion of the harem for family use, embroidery workshops have been mentioned by visitors to Turkey, who also suggested that some Turkish women sold their embroideries through an agent in the souks.

The Turks were Sunni Moslems and allowed no representations of humans or animals in their decoration, although these rules were sometimes relaxed to allow the use of floral forms. Consequently many designs show stylised plants, flowers, leaves and fruit.

The most fascinating aspect of this particular sash is the use of pattern and colour; in the bunches of grapes the richness of metal linked with the lustre of silk is particularly effective. The simplicity of the pattern of squares and lines belies its potential for development – changes in technique, scale of pattern, even the proportions within the pattern can create a multiplicity of contemporary interpretations.

Initial research began with painting and drawing in order to explore the pattern's potential. Experiments included print grid patterns, collages of torn/cut paper squares, discharging the pattern using bleach, and graffito techniques. By cutting and rearranging the results, shapes for garments and designs for panels emerged, creating a link between the original idea and the development.

At this stage, a collection of hand-embroidered samples were made, which included blocks of silk stitchery; gold purls in squares with couched lines and vice versa; variations of *or nué*; canvaswork with ribbons; reverse appliqué with transparent fabrics; and on a larger scale, patchwork with printed textured squares.

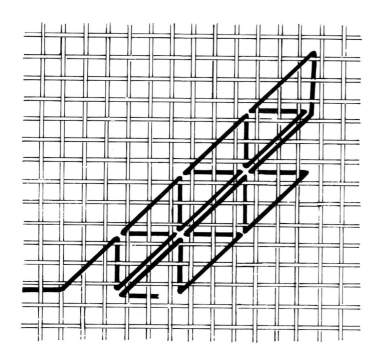

*Musabak stitch showing first stage of reverse faggot
followed by single faggot worked over first stage*
(DRAWING: MOLLIE PICKEN)

Printing the pattern on fabric, and using fabric crayons for rubbings of grids, were direct developments from the printed paper ones. The pattern was embellished by adding squares of dyed/painted fabric with a grid worked with straight machine stitching. The result suggested a background fabric for garments and accessories, and variations on this idea led to further developments.

Weaving gold paper strips with a coloured edge resulted in a distortion of the grid; and further folded paperwork in a three-dimensional step design led to the same structure being worked on a small scale in felt, with machine embroidery interlaced with a thick purple silk. Other experiments included grids of machine-made cords; purple silk grids machined on gold-painted felt; and machine-embroidered samples in whip, satin and straight stitches to re-create the diagonal lines of the original square.

Selecting and discarding ideas is important before deciding on the final design. A sketchbook of notes and experiments suggested a three-dimensional rather than a flat approach. The firmness pro-

duced by dense machining on felt incorporating areas of foil, gave a structural quality which suited free-standing forms.

Taking this idea further, a vessel was constructed, wider at the top and tapering towards the base, and a machine-made cord grid was overlaid on the background to echo the pattern of the original Turkish embroidery. A separate smaller-scale grid stiffened with thin wire was made, and this can be superimposed on the vessel in a variety of ways.

Developing the pattern and retaining the colour scheme has interpreted the spirit of the Turkish embroidery, while its reversible nature has been captured by the use of a sculptured form.

CHAPTER TWENTY-FIVE

SHIFTING COLOUR

Christine Cooper

THE TENT HANGING illustrated comes from
the central Asian area known as Turkestan,
which for many centuries was inhabited
by a tribe of nomadic people called the Turkmen.
Their homes were large tents (yurts) that had a
framework of folding lattice-work sides with a
domed roof covered with large pieces of thick wool
felt. The interior of the tent was very colourful, with
storage bags of different sizes in either kelim weave
(fine, flat woven carpet type) or knotted fabrics,
hung round the tent sides. One or two patchwork
curtains might be hung on the wall opposite the
door, and these would also be used to decorate the
flanks of the bridal camel in a wedding procession or
when travelling. Wealthy families would drape the
tent ceiling with printed fabrics from Russia.

The immediate impression of the tent hanging is
of a patchwork of squares and triangles arranged
within borders. Closer study shows that within this
broad description there is a wealth of interesting detail, not only in the variation of method but in the
type of fabric used, and the size and placing of the
shapes. The hanging shows three very different
techniques: patchwork, ikat weaving and cross stitch
embroidery.

The squares of fabric in the centre and the red
squares in the surrounding border have a brushed or
felted surface; these are edged with a narrow black
cotton fabric. The green squares are velvet, edged

*Patchwork tent hanging from Afghanistan using pieced
ikat cloth separated by narrow, patterned, cross-
stitched borders*
EG no 9; 1983; 101 x 100cm (40 x 39¹/₂in)
(PHOTOGRAPHY: DUDLEY MOSS)

with strips of various colours. Ikat cloth, together with some plain silks, is used in the triangles. Throughout the hanging all the borders are added in the manner of log-cabin patchwork.

There are many variations of pattern within the cross stitch borders. The overall impression is of a composition of triangles, but sometimes what appears to be a straightforward sequence of colour, changes almost imperceptibly to another variation and includes borders with little fat crosses and variations on double hook or 'S' shapes. The stitches are worked in a floss silk thread, on a cotton background fabric. Many colours have been used, echoing the remnants of ikat cloth and ranging through the colour spectrum from yellow to purple.

The remnants of ikat cloth used for the fabric triangles comprise an important part of the hanging. Larger pieces of ikat are used for the outer borders, and one can begin to see some of the fascinating patterns made by this method. Ikat is a traditional method of patterning yarn by binding and dyeing the warp before weaving to create 'resist' patterns. Over the centuries it has spread to most continents of the world, developing in a variety of ways. Turkestan was one area where the method became highly developed, being produced as long ago as the eighth century AD, and these cloths were made in workshops in oases and towns. They were made of silk or silk and cotton, and used for table and bed coverings, wall hangings, cushions and clothing. It is possible that the tantalising glimpses of ikat patterns in the triangles and outer borders of this hanging were left over from the production of such items.

At the beginning of this century, cheap printed cotton fabrics were imported from Russia, almost ending the production of traditional fabrics. Many Turkmen weavers emigrated to Afghanistan, hoping to continue weaving their highly ornamented fabrics; but most of them were unable to develop a market. However, a few continued to work in Afghanistan, producing simpler designs woven in cotton or synthetic fibres and coloured with chemical dyes. By allowing the dyes to seep under the bindings and soften the edges of the colour changes, the weavers developed cloths of glowing, blended colours.

It is the shifting colour of the ikat fabrics that

An impression in pastels of an ikat pattern similar to those in the hanging. Triangles added as contrast
(PHOTOGRAPHY: JIM PASCOE)

(right) *Long fabric strips in four colours joined to form a deep band, with free machining worked with invisible thread in needle and frequent colour changes on spool*
(PHOTOGRAPHY: JIM PASCOE)

helps to give this piece its liveliness, and it was this aspect which I decided to explore. Various colouring media were applied to paper in random overlapping bands to simulate the ikat effect; the most successful were soft oil and chalk pastels used separately and to-

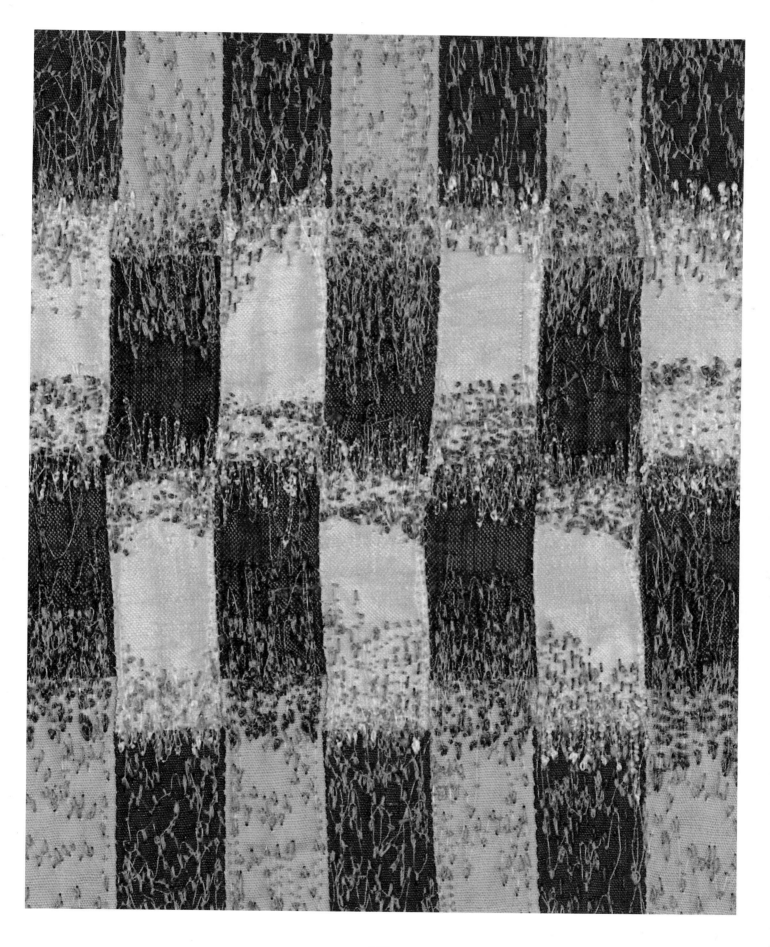

gether, in various ways. Further areas of colour were then cut up and re-assembled to form new patterns, and I found that bands of colour offset against each other worked best.

These experiments led to a series of samples using the Seminole patchwork technique, with the seams softened by stitching. However, more variation came from joining fabric strips of varying lengths individually rather than in the traditional Seminole way. Overlaid fabrics were bonded together and stitched into, and in order to keep the richness of the original textile, close tones were often used instead of just one colour. I also considered adding gold in thread, print and fabric, as line or triangles, to highlight areas of the pieces.

These experiments suggested the idea for the bag. Two sets of strips were joined end to end, reversing and offsetting the colours to change both pattern and direction. Free machining with a coloured thread on the bobbin and invisible thread in the needle, was worked over much of the surface to soften the joins, and this resulted in the bonus of a rich texture. I had intended to apply small silk triangles to the front but they were not suitable, so they were used in a simple arrangement on the back.

As it was too difficult to turn the stepped edges neatly, I found the solution was to machine satin stitch in metallic thread across the top of both sections of the bag with the lining in place. The sections were joined with satin stitching down the sides and across the base. I made fine, multi-coloured twisted cords and tassels and attached them by hand. The little hollow balls added to the base are similar to the decorations used in Turkmen jewellery and artefacts of the nineteenth century.

Other ways of interpreting the ikat pattern suggested themselves during the working of this piece. Fine cords, narrow ribbons, metallic and thick, glossy threads could be hand-couched onto a rich background fabric and experiments could be made with thicker cords and threads. Also, dense areas of machine stitching with shiny threads could be used to blend rich coloured fabrics together.

Chalk pastels used on their sides to give the impression of the shifting colours of ikat pattern
(DRAWING: CHRISTINE COOPER. PHOTOGRAPHY: JIM PASCOE)

(opposite) *Front of bag. Variation of Seminole patchwork taking the ikat fabrics as inspiration and the colour scheme from one of the paper experiments. Free machine embroidery softens the edges of the fabric strips. Designed and worked by Christine Cooper*
(PHOTOGRAPHY: JIM PASCOE)

CHAPTER TWENTY-SIX

INDIAN STORY

Jean Draper

THE NAME RUMAL (meaning handkerchief), is given to small cloth covers from India, which may be decorated with painting, printing or embroidery. This illustration of a fine nineteenth-century example from the Embroiderers' Guild Collection, is typical of the classical Chamba rumal – Chamba being a small kingdom in the Punjab Hills. The restraint and skill in drawing and stitchery suggests that it could have been embroidered by ladies of the court.

The rumal is worked on natural-coloured fine cotton, the edges bound with terracotta-coloured silk. Where some of the stitchery is missing, the fine outline drawing in earth-red paint can be observed. Formal floral bands, drawn with rhythm and delicacy, are used as borders and to separate the four pictorial panels which depict episodes from the life of the God Krishna. The principal scene shows Radha visiting her lover Krishna, carrying an offering of a garland. He awaits her within a curtained chamber, reclining on a decorative carpet and cushion. The other pictures show Krishna playing with friends, some of whom are hidden in a tree; Krishna and followers preparing for battle; and Radha waiting in a bower. Krishna can be identified by his blue skin colouring.

The design is outlined in double running stitch in black silk, then embroidered in small double-darning stitch in floss silk in cream, yellow, orange, green, soft brown and blue. The stitchery gives a soft, flat, even appearance on both sides of the cloth. In some places, especially on the floral borders, the black outlining has been overlapped by the darning and partly obliterated. The resulting softened edge gives the motifs a curious three-dimensional quality, as if floating above the background. Variations in the dyes used for the silks give additional colour interest.

In some places where the silk stitchery is worn away, the fabric shows a lighter colour and needle marks are apparent in the outline. Tarnished silver-gilt plate emphasises garment details and some of the floral motifs.

Rumals were highly valued as offerings for deities and officials, as gifts exchanged between the families of the bride and bridegroom at weddings, and as covers to protect other gifts or precious objects from heat and dust. Sometimes they were hung above an altar or behind an idol. Although rectangular ones do exist, rumals were usually square in shape and the decoration was designed to be seen from all sides. The layout, as in this example, usually consists of floral borders enclosing finely drawn figurative scenes inspired by lyrical poetry, mythology and the legends of Krishna.

Embroidered rumals were produced in the Pahari Hill States of Punjab, now known as Himachal Pradesh. From the eighteenth century onwards, these embroideries were made so abundantly and to such a high standard in Chamba, that the title 'Chamba Rumal' is often attributed to all similar work from the whole region. During the reign of the Mughal emperors there was great encouragement of the arts and Mughal influence on painting at the Pahari courts was particularly strong. The embroidered rumals reflect the style of these miniature paintings and also the mural paintings which decorated the 'Painted Palace', the residence of the ladies of the Chamba court. Often the drawing is so skilful and sophisticated that it is supposed that the court painters assisted in the initial planning of the embroidery, which could well have been the case with

Study-sheet of drawings from rumal showing Krishna, Radha, floral and tree forms (DRAWINGS: JEAN DRAPER)

this example. (Another rumal, also in the Embroiderers' Guild collection, is by comparison, much more primitive both in drawing and stitchery, indicating that it could be the work of a village woman.)

The overall quality of this embroidery is elegant, sensitive and subtle in treatment. In colour and in the design of the floral motifs used, it is reminiscent of Mughal architectural decoration, most notably inlay work in semi-precious stones. Despite the pictorial nature of the embroidery and its undoubted links with the contemporary painting of the period, the work remains a fine example of an embroidered textile in the purest sense. It is never a mere imitation painting.

The study of the embroidery, which began as an exciting project for this book, has brought about a radical change in my work. The rumal was initially allocated to me because of my interest in Indian textiles, and particularly tribal embroideries which have often been a source of inspiration for my work. Although it was different from anything studied before, the rumal appealed immediately although the figurative characteristics gave cause for misgivings. Two days were spent studying the embroidery, drawing, reading for information and taking photographs for reference.

I considered several possible ways of developing contemporary work based on the rumal; these included the investigation of the double darning technique, changing the scale and direction. Samples of soft, glossy surface textures and patterns were made; quilting designs were developed from the rhythmic, floral borders, keeping the design and colour qualities understated. The Indian flower, tree and architectural forms were also considered as starting-points for design.

Until this point the figurative element had been

Study-board showing drawings of flowers from Indian textiles; drawings of Indian women carrying water-pots; stitched samples with variations of running and darning stitches in floss silks, and combinations of machine-stitchery, hand-stitchery and appliqué; floral prints and stencils (DRAWINGS: JEAN DRAPER)

ignored, but now it was time to meet the challenge head-on. There were several subject matters which could be explored, ranging from Krishna/Hindu legends, Indian lovers from miniature paintings, lovers in legends from cultures other than Indian, and legendary figures of Anglo-Saxon or Celtic origin.

Suitable floss threads were assembled, and investigations were made into the availability of pure silk and more economical substitutes. After these preliminaries, some stitch samples were begun: initially I found double darning in floss silk was quite difficult, but with practice it improved. This technique was most successful on an open Indian

Cover for a ceremonial gift (rumal). The background fabric is fine cotton, embroidered with coloured silks, using closely worked fillings of double-darning stitch, with details in silver flat wire. The design is of four figurative panels, depicting episodes from the life of the God Krishna
EG no 3263; nineteenth century; 76.5cm (30in) square. Donor unknown (PHOTOGRAPHY: DUDLEY MOSS)

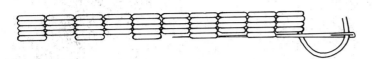

Double darning stitch   (DRAWING: MOLLIE PICKEN)

Hand-stitched sampler. Double darning and other darning developments in a variety of floss silks on fine Indian cotton   (PHOTOGRAPHY: JEAN DRAPER)

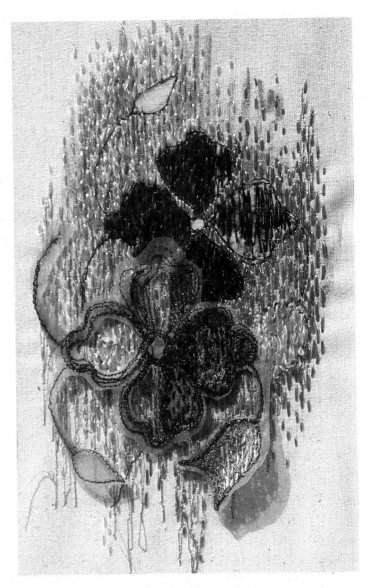

Sampler combining machine- and hand-stitchery. A variety of threads can be used on the top of the machine for free swing-needle and tacking stitchery. Designed and worked by Jean Draper   (PHOTOGRAPHY: JEAN DRAPER)

cotton, held in a frame, with an outline worked first to control the stitchery, as in the original. I decided that an extended range of darning treatments, perhaps in conjunction with machining, fabric painting and printing, were more appropriate for contemporary work.

This project coincided with a second trip to India which was a great help. Whilst in India I noticed and was excited by different aspects of the country, probably as a result of studying the rumal. My attention began to focus on people, particularly women and children in everyday situations, and on flower forms which are used in decoration on textiles and architecture. Drawings were made and photographs taken for future reference.

At home, further drawings were made and some tentative figure and flower embroideries were begun. I experienced great difficulty with the figurative work because of a number of convictions, principally that the work must not copy the rumal or any other Indian art form, but must be an honest personal statement. I also felt that the figures must be well drawn but not contain too much detail, and that they should emerge from the background fabric. The intrinsic textile quality should be predominant. Thus, the fascinating challenge of interpreting figures continues.

Finished work incorporating figure, floral and architectural forms. Machine- and hand-stitchery on cotton, organdie and dissolvable fabrics. Paint and handmade paper. Designed and worked by Jean Draper (PHOTOGRAPHY: JEAN DRAPER)

CHAPTER TWENTY-SEVEN

BANDS OF COLOUR

Dorothy Sim

THE TROUSER CUFF illustrated is from north-west India or Pakistan, and dates from the late nineteenth or early twentieth century. It is made of light green sateen and decorated with small formalised floral motifs 4.5 x 3cm ($1^{3}/_{4}$ x $1^{1}/_{8}$in) worked in gilt twist couched down with silk. These are underlined at the hem by a wide border – 10cm (4in) – of gilt twist, couched into formalised

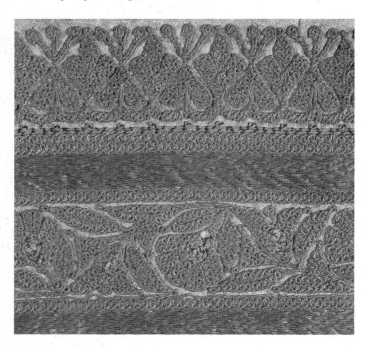

Detail of trouser cuff   (PHOTOGRAPHY: DUDLEY MOSS)

(right) *Trouser cuff from north-west India or Pakistan, decorated with small formalised floral motifs worked in gilt twist couched down with silk*
EG no 184 1983; late nineteenth–early twentieth century; 35 x 22cm ($14^{1}/_{2}$ x 9in) narrowing to 14cm ($5^{1}/_{2}$in)   (PHOTOGRAPHY: DUDLEY MOSS)

Map of north-west India showing where the embroidery originated

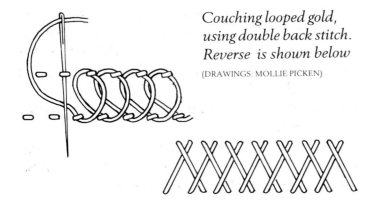

Couching looped gold, using double back stitch. Reverse is shown below

(DRAWINGS: MOLLIE PICKEN)

floral patterns separated by a broad band of gold passing thread, couched to show a chevron pattern. The small motifs are worked directly onto the green sateen with no backing material to the embroidery, and the hem edge of the cuff is finished with a piece of commercially manufactured braid gimp. Gilt-twist thread is couched down with orange silk using double back-stitch over the looped twist, and completely fills the motif. The curls at the foot and top of the motifs change to simple couching, and the small

166

central area of the motif is in silver twist couched with purple silk.

A backing of white cotton material lines the solidly worked wide sateen border (border width 10cm [4in]). In addition to the same style of looped couching, held with double back stitch, and plain couched gold twist, there is also silver-gilt twist, couched in lines with purple silk thread; gold passing thread is couched with red silk to form a chevron pattern about 1cm ($\frac{1}{2}$in) in width. At no point is the gilt or silver thread taken to the reverse side of the sateen material.

The embroidery and materials have a certain lack of sophistication, and although very attractive, this would suggest that the work was probably the product of a smaller workshop. So that as little as possible of the embroidery was wasted in the cutting of the garment, the gilt embroidery was worked across a piece of sateen, and the required shape of the trouser cuff cut to fit it.

The repeating motif pattern would be stamped on the material with a wooden block, and in places a line of yellow paint can be seen echoing the pattern. A commercially manufactured gimp at the base of the cuff suggests a date in the early part of the twentieth century. However, the patterns and designs used, even in the twentieth century, are a continuation of those employed in an ancient craft, going back to the lavish gold and silver embroidery patronised by the Moghul Court.

Techniques for preparing the cloth to be embroidered are common throughout the region. Women take their cloth to the local 'chapager' or block printer who stamps out their chosen patterns. The cloth is then stretched taut over a frame and is ready for embroidery, which is most likely to be done by men. These patterns will vary within the region, each area having its own tradition.

Pakistan and north-west India have produced cotton cloth since at least 500BC, and of a fine quality, often up to sixty threads to the inch/2.5cm. It is an area also recognised as being well advanced in the techniques of mordant and resist dyeing. Generally, animal fibres take natural dyes easily, whereas vegetable fibres (eg cotton) only take certain dyes and it is often a lengthier process.

The cuff at the base of decorated trousers would show when worn beneath a tunic shirt or dress, and the decoration would possibly echo that on a small jacket worn over the tunic. Thus, as the original piece was part of a costume, a small panel was planned as a development, with the view to using it as a resource sample for fashion embroidery. This could be developed into an accessory such as a scarf or bag, or part of the pattern could be used for embellishing a luxurious garment.

In the original, pattern bands of goldwork are worked in tight and painstaking couching techniques. For this modern piece however, the plan was to keep to the goldwork theme but to emphasise the colours used for the couching threads in the original, developing and enlarging the patterns and couching styles using modern materials and techniques. A Thai silk material in similar colour to the original was chosen for a background, and was backed with fine cotton material.

Developing the floral band pattern was the first step. This was scaled up, and the colour of the original couching emphasised by using a red and gold tissue cut into shapes and bonded to the background with a transfer fusing web. To echo the original looping design these shapes were held in place by Pekinese stitch, and the background colour softened by the use of random couching with gold thread.

The double back stitch couching of the original which produced the looping effect was worked on a much larger scale. A cord was made by machine-wrapping string with a zig-zag stitch in multi-coloured metallic thread. This cord was made over several different thicknesses of core, and two of these were used in the curved banding at the top of the patterns and at the hem of the sample.

Machine embroidery on dissolvable fabric over net was used for the individual motifs and parts of the underlying pattern. To give a rich effect, flat bands of couching were made by stitching down metallic ribbon in two widths. The smaller samples show alternative beginnings for pattern bands using two metallics.

Many variations can be made on these deceptively simple couching methods. Colour and gold can be used to create jewel-like bands of pattern.

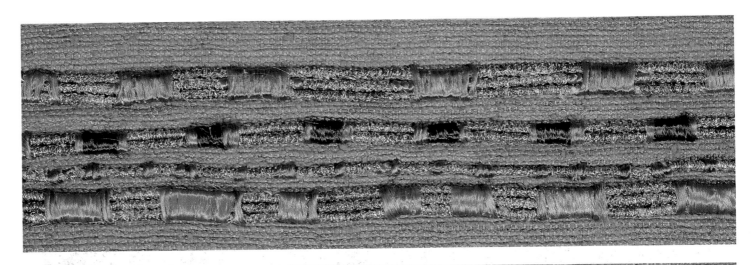

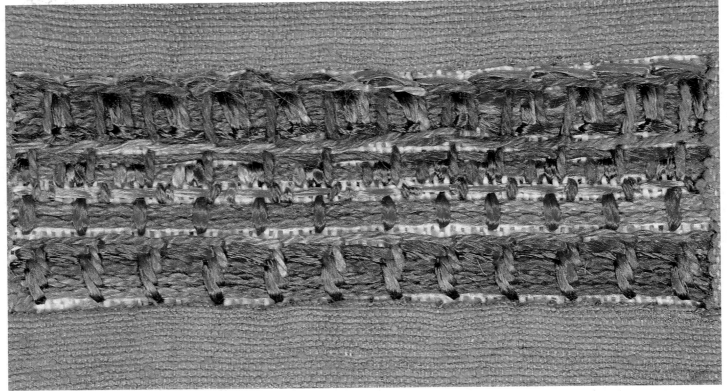

(top) *Sample showing possibilities of machine- and hand-wrapping fine string to make a braided thread for couching. This technique gives an added firmness to the background material and would be excellent for belts, cuffs, purses etc. Designed and worked by Dorothy Sim* (PHOTOGRAPHY: PETER READ)

(bottom) *Sample showing bands of couching using a variety of stitches to hold down background thread. In this sample the couching almost completely obscures the background of evenweave material. Designed and worked by Dorothy Sim* (PHOTOGRAPHY: PETER READ)

(right) *A contemporary development of the original piece illustrating how it has been adapted using modern techniques of machine embroidery and bonding. Designed and worked by Dorothy Sim* (PHOTOGRAPHY: PETER READ)

CHAPTER TWENTY-EIGHT

FROM PEACOCK TO COPE

Jane Lemon

THE UNIQUE COLLAR illustrated here came from a box containing fragments of art embroideries which had been cut up to make decoration for dress. It is likely that the collar was made from a larger, circular-shaped piece as there are two small 'shoulder darts' which have transformed it with speed and little expertise to its present shape. The jap gold is of a warm reddish shade which is reinforced by the brown silk core breaking through in many places, and the coiling, flowing movement of the design forms units which build up into a solid band.

A Chinese influence is evident in the treatment of these cloud scrolls – in fact the piece might well be Chinese. The motif could have been removed from an original robe, possibly to form part of the decoration of a Chinese theatrical costume of the nineteenth century. However, the quality and flowing movement of the scrolls are not followed through in the more static drawing of the peacock feathers which radiate to the outer edge.

The feathers are worked in a not-too-perfect satin stitch, using a single thread of yellow and green silk twisted together. The cream silk satin background is completely covered with stitching except for the eye of each feather where a paillette or jewel appears to have been removed. Although the movement of the gold thread is the most interesting technique in the embroidery, it is the use of the peacock feather motif which gives the design its character. The collar measures 70cm (27½in) long on the outside edge and 41cm (16in) long on the inside. It is 5.5cm (2⅛in) deep at the centre back and 5cm (2in) deep at the front edge. One can only guess that the piece was embroidered during the last quarter of the nineteenth century, and worn in its present form in the 1920s or early 1930s.

The spark of excitement which led me to study this collar as a basis for future work came not from the indifferent stitching, but from the peacock as a design source. Peacock motifs occur throughout history, in carved, painted or woven forms, so it is hardly surprising that it is an inspiration for the embroiderer. In ancient Rome the peacock became a symbol of immortality because its flesh was believed to be incorruptible. Later in early Christian belief it became a symbol of the resurrection. Then with the spreading of Christianity, the peacock symbol was adopted by ethnic European embroideries, particularly in Assisi-work.

Having established that the peacock motif was acceptable as a Christian symbol, I was thus able to consider using it to decorate ecclesiastical vestments, an area of particular interest for me. My first thought on looking at the feathers on the collar in this light, was that enlarged and elongated, the design would fill a cope or chasuble shape very happily; on further reflection however, it seemed to me to resemble a Maori cloak or an African tribal chief's ceremonial cape, and was therefore not at all suitable. However, being aware of the possibilities of changing the scale, I decided that the motif would either fill the area on one cope panel, form a border panel for an orphrey, or could be reduced to a jewelled detail on a morse.

As the vestments have to be viewed from a distance, it is important that the design forms good strong shapes. Tone and texture play a vital part in a successful design for this situation, and colour needs to provide impact from a distance so that the vestment shows up against the background of the building in which it is to be used. However beautiful, a

Peacock motifs from various sources
(DRAWINGS: JANE LEMON)

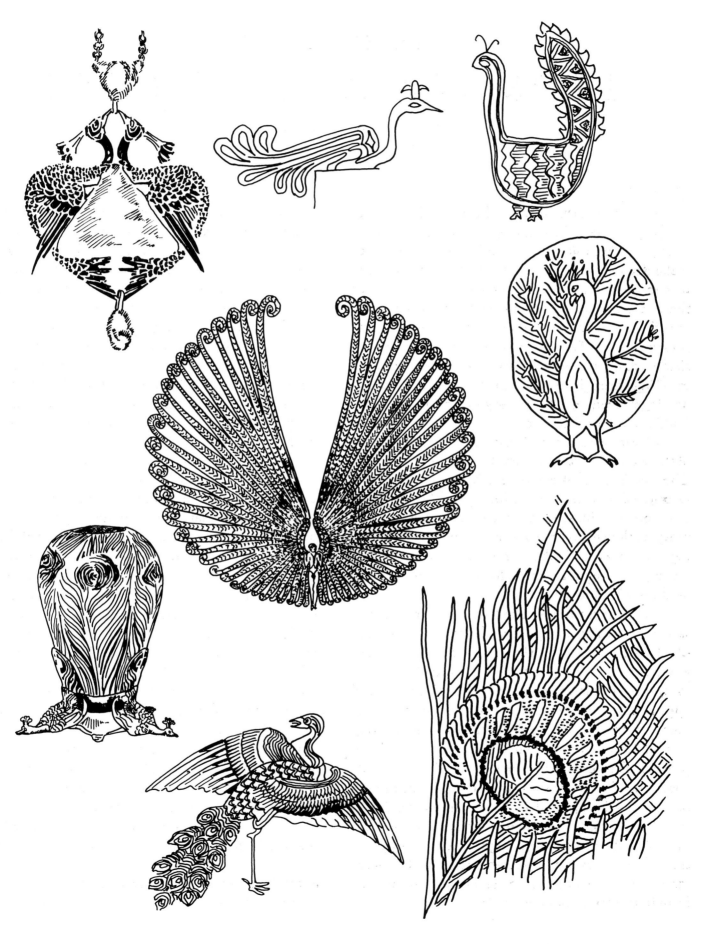

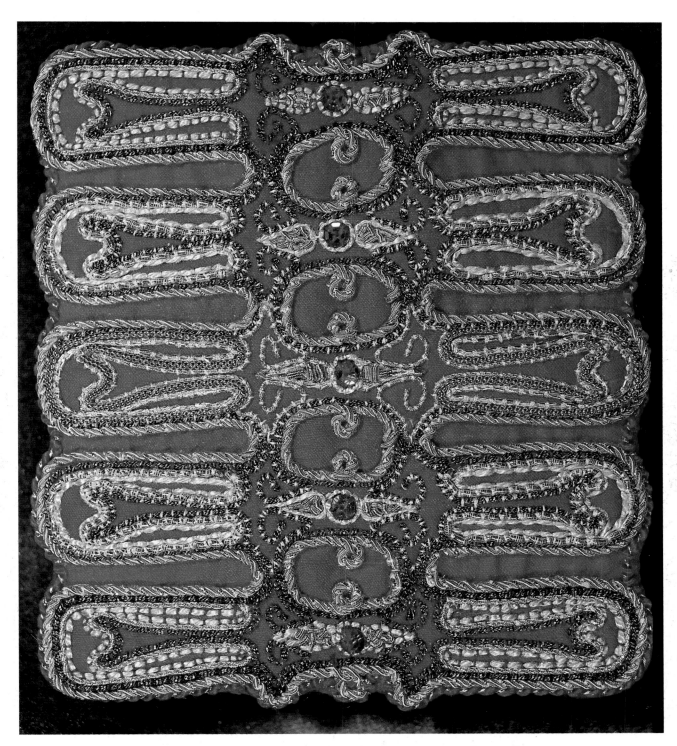

(left) *Collar with peacock feather design worked in couched jap gold*
Un-numbered; 70 x 41cm (27¹/₂in x 16¹/₄in)
(PHOTOGRAPHY: DUDLEY MOSS)

The original unit has been duplicated and mirrored to form a design suitable for a morse (fastening for a cope). It is worked in metal threads, with the padding increasing in height towards the centre. Coloured threads have been used with the metal to accentuate the movement of the gold, and the tones lightened to give a central highlight. Designed and worked by Jane Lemon (PHOTOGRAPHY: PETER READ)

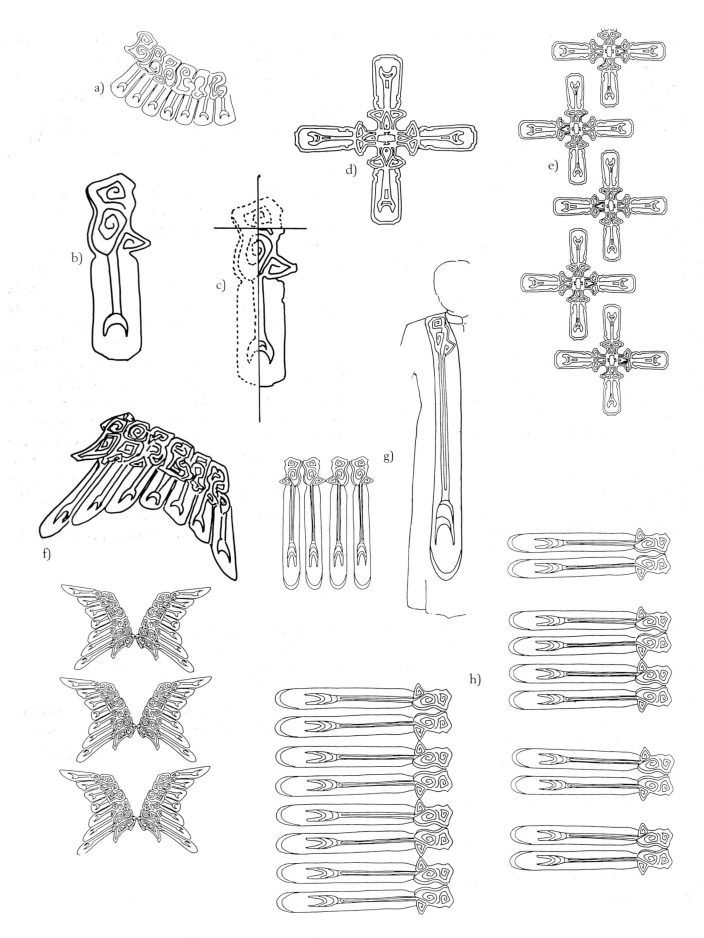

cream or pale-blue cope can disappear against the stonework in a cathedral. Moreover, since vestments are expected to last for many years, far longer than any secular garment, the best available fabrics and threads are used.

The cope, a ceremonial vestment used in procession, needs to be dignified, have a good shape and move well; as it hangs in folds, the design must be appropriate. Vestments are designed to be seen in movement on the human form, so the cut is all-important. The historic half-circle cope is extremely uncomfortable to wear as it is inclined to fall backwards, choking the wearer with the morse, the clasp which fastens the front together on the chest. This problem can be solved if the cope is cut with shoulder darts to make the garment well balanced and comfortable.

The placing of the decoration is important and heavy embroidery should be restricted to the area below the chin line, approximately 7.5–10cm (3–4in) below the neckline so that it will not rub. Similarly it should not be used where the hands may be clasped at waist level, nor on the lower back where it might be sat upon.

For my contemporary interpretation of the Embroiderers' Guild example I decided to apply the peacock feather motif to a design for a morse. I began drawing up a section of the collar simplifying the movement of the gold thread to show its general direction. This could then be traced, overlaid, reversed or distorted to produce patterns (a process which can be done on a computer in a fraction of the time). If different sizes of the same motif are used in building up a design, photocopiers can help with the previously tedious job of enlarging or reducing the size.

Two design units were placed next to each other, and mirrored to form a design suitable for a morse. A rich, jewelled effect was achieved by working the embroidery in metal threads, with the padding increasing in height towards the centre. Coloured threads have been used with the metal to accentuate the movement of the gold, and the tones lightened to give a central highlight. The finished embroidery was mounted over plywood, which was cut to shape and padded with felt and the back covered with gloving leather. Before the embroidery was mounted two holes were made in the wood and a strip of leather passed through so that the morse could be applied easily to a band of stiffened fabric to attach it to the cope. In the past, the fastenings on copes were silver, gold or jewelled clasps, but the decorated bars on modern ones do not have the same solidity. The plywood adds weight and distinction to the embroidery, which gives a decorative importance to the morse.

DESIGN DEVELOPMENTS

a) Drawings of the shapes in the original embroidery
b) One unit isolated
c) A section of the unit selected as the basis of the design development
d) The section mirrored, developed and repeated to form a cross. The cross can be used on a stole, burse or veil in its present form, but if it is required in a larger size for a chasuble the detail within the design needs to be built up
e) The cross used as a unit to form an orphrey for a chasuble
f) By distorting a section of the original drawing of the collar, a shape resembling an angel's wing has appeared. Placed in pairs, these can build into a variety of orphrey designs

g) By distorting the original single unit, a design for a stole end has been produced. Using it in a large scale makes an interesting broad stole which can be worn with a cassock-alb
h) The same distorted unit is used in a small scale to build into a strong pattern for a cope orphrey, used either as a solid pattern or in blocks of varying widths
(DRAWINGS: JANE LEMON)

CHAPTER TWENTY-NINE

MYSTERIES OF A CHINESE JACKET

Mary Youles

THE JACKET shown is made of navy shot silk satin, with a centre front opening, applied loops, and buttons of knotted fabric. There are scattered flowers embroidered in knots, and the rest of the stitchery is in variations of satin stitch. Symbolic motifs include butterflies, cherry blossom, chrysanthemums, water, clouds, rocks, mountains and swastika crosses.

The jacket has short sleeves, with extra sleeve-bands of yellow silk, woven in warp-faced satin and covered in rich embroidery. These bands are badly worn, and are now held in place by tacking to the lining. The neck and edges have two applied borders, one of which is a black band decorated with flowers and bats; it appears to be stiffened at the back with a paste or glue. A narrow woven ribbon has been

added at a later stage, in some places obscuring the embroidery. It is attached with crude tacking stitches.

The lining is a plain weave, with silk filaments dyed in a subtle 'greyed' range of blues, possibly using vegetable dyes. Extra pieces have been added at the side vents to increase the width of the hem, and close inspection reveals two sets of four flower heads woven into the cloth in twill patterning. This may suggest that the lining is rather special, and has been taken from an earlier garment.

There is a similar jacket in the Victoria & Albert Museum in London, without the intriguing yellow sleeve-bands. Verity Wilson illustrates this jacket in her book *Chinese Dress*, and tells us that such robes could be purchased off the peg; it is therefore reasonable to assume that similar garments may have been made in the same workshop.

During the Qing dynasty (1644–1912) the Han

Textured stitches from the reverse side of the embroidery, drawn from inside the jacket. There is no sign of the colours fading. The stitchery is less smooth and perfect than the front but equally beautiful
(DRAWING: MARY YOULES)

(left) *A Han Chinese jacket, in navy silk satin. The embroidery is worked in knots and variations of satin stitch*
EG Handling Collection (no accession number); 65 x 126cm (25½ x 49¾in); late nineteenth century
(PHOTOGRAPHY: DUDLEY MOSS)

CHINESE JACKET SUGGESTED JOURNEYS OF EXPLORATION

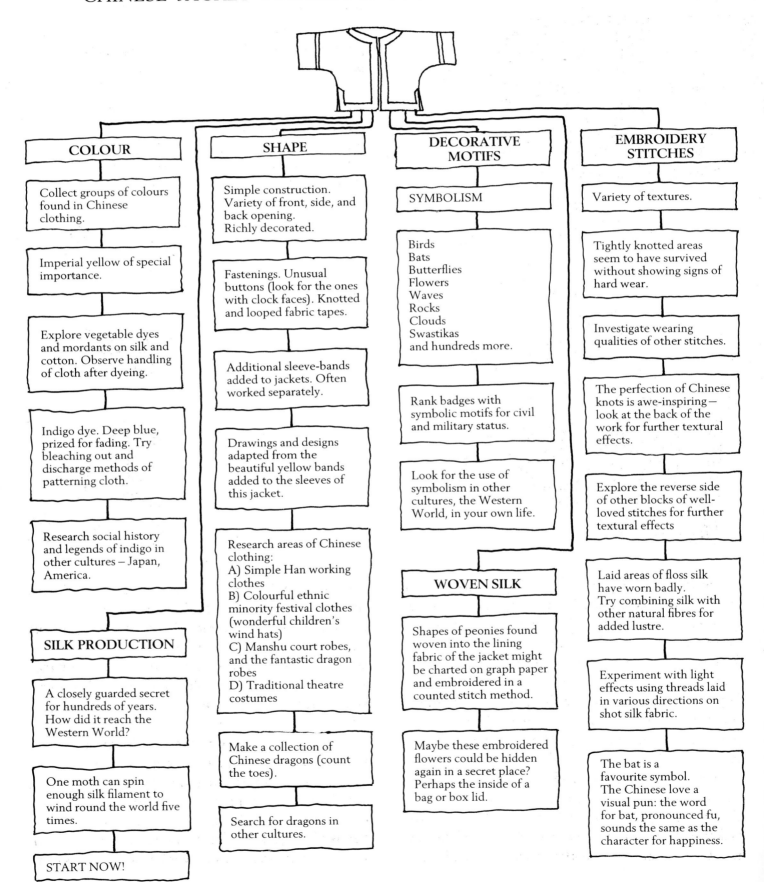

COLOUR

Collect groups of colours found in Chinese clothing.

Imperial yellow of special importance.

Explore vegetable dyes and mordants on silk and cotton. Observe handling of cloth after dyeing.

Indigo dye. Deep blue, prized for fading. Try bleaching out and discharge methods of patterning cloth.

Research social history and legends of indigo in other cultures – Japan, America.

SILK PRODUCTION

A closely guarded secret for hundreds of years. How did it reach the Western World?

One moth can spin enough silk filament to wind round the world five times.

START NOW!

SHAPE

Simple construction. Variety of front, side, and back opening. Richly decorated.

Fastenings. Unusual buttons (look for the ones with clock faces). Knotted and looped fabric tapes.

Additional sleeve-bands added to jackets. Often worked separately.

Drawings and designs adapted from the beautiful yellow bands added to the sleeves of this jacket.

Research areas of Chinese clothing:
A) Simple Han working clothes
B) Colourful ethnic minority festival clothes (wonderful children's wind hats)
C) Manshu court robes, and the fantastic dragon robes
D) Traditional theatre costumes

Make a collection of Chinese dragons (count the toes).

Search for dragons in other cultures.

DECORATIVE MOTIFS

SYMBOLISM

Birds
Bats
Butterflies
Flowers
Waves
Rocks
Clouds
Swastikas
and hundreds more.

Rank badges with symbolic motifs for civil and military status.

Look for the use of symbolism in other cultures, the Western World, in your own life.

WOVEN SILK

Shapes of peonies found woven into the lining fabric of the jacket might be charted on graph paper and embroidered in a counted stitch method.

Maybe these embroidered flowers could be hidden again in a secret place? Perhaps the inside of a bag or box lid.

EMBROIDERY STITCHES

Variety of textures.

Tightly knotted areas seem to have survived without showing signs of hard wear.

Investigate wearing qualities of other stitches.

The perfection of Chinese knots is awe-inspiring — look at the back of the work for further textural effects.

Explore the reverse side of other blocks of well-loved stitches for further textural effects

Laid areas of floss silk have worn badly. Try combining silk with other natural fibres for added lustre.

Experiment with light effects using threads laid in various directions on shot silk fabric.

The bat is a favourite symbol. The Chinese love a visual pun: the word for bat, pronounced fu, sounds the same as the character for happiness.

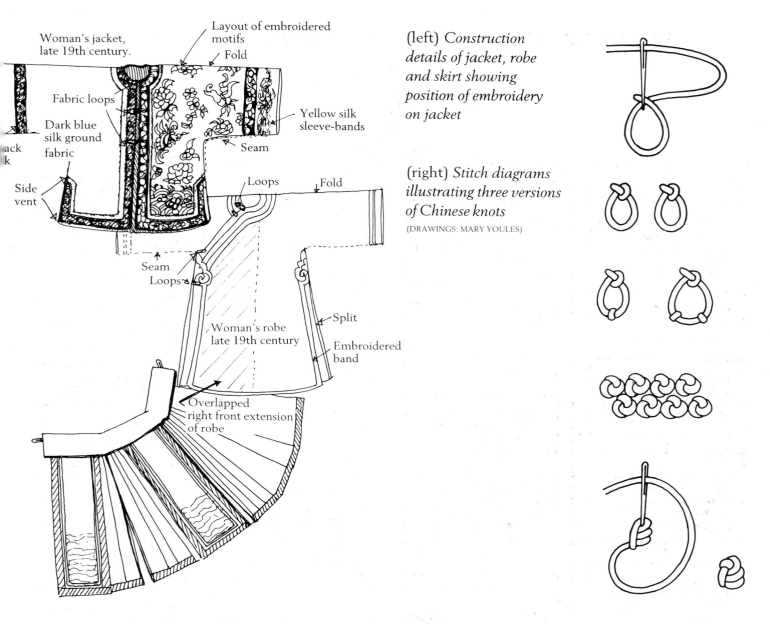

Woman's jacket, late 19th century.

Layout of embroidered motifs

Fold

Fabric loops

Yellow silk sleeve-bands

Dark blue silk ground fabric

Seam

Side vent

Loops

Fold

Seam

Loops

Split

Woman's robe late 19th century

Embroidered band

Overlapped right front extension of robe

ack k

(left) *Construction details of jacket, robe and skirt showing position of embroidery on jacket*

(right) *Stitch diagrams illustrating three versions of Chinese knots*
(DRAWINGS: MARY YOULES)

Chinese, who formed the majority of the population, were ruled by the Manchu people. They had different styles of dress: Manchu women generally wore a long robe with sleeves and curved cuffs, and Han women wore a shorter robe or jacket with wide sleeves, over a skirt; several layers of trousers or leggings were worn under the skirt. The garments were worn loose so they would rustle and swing. This, rather than the shape they revealed was considered erotic.

Han skirts and robes were, to Western eyes, usually in clashing colours and thus may help to explain the addition of the two yellow sleeve-bands on the jacket, which seem unrelated to the rest of the garment. They may be of earlier origin, particularly as

they are now considerably more fragmented than other parts of the jacket. Yellow was a colour associated with the Imperial Court, and it is possible that there could be a connection. Verity Wilson suggests that Chinese embroidered sleeve-bands sometimes served a similar purpose to European samplers, as many were never used, and others were left unfinished.

Many thousands of decorative designs had symbolic meanings: during the nineteenth century pattern books of approved styles were printed, using woodblocks on thin paper sheets which were traced or pounced onto the cloth. On the yellow sleeve-bands of the jacket, a fine black line can just be seen, where the embroidery has worn away. Stencils were

A wall-hanging based on the shape of the jacket. Frayed silk scraps were bonded and machine-stitched to a dark blue felt backing. Applied shapes symbolising water were worked separately. The yellow sleeve-bands are hand and machine embroidered to enrich the surface. Designed and worked by Mary Youles

(PHOTOGRAPHY: JIM PASCOE)

Drawing of yellow silk sleeve-band, very worn and darned, showing parts of the blue/grey lining. Changes of stitch direction catch the light effectively

(DRAWING: MARY YOULES)

Detail of wall-hanging
(PHOTOGRAPHY: JIM PASCOE)

The name 'Turkestan' appeared in the sixteenth century and became the generally accepted term for this vast area, although the name was later abolished by the Soviets. It is a region with a very ancient urban cultural tradition, and towns such as Samarkand, Bukhara and Merv were of great importance when Eastern Islam was at the height of its powers. These settlements depended on the nomadic caravans to sell and exchange their wares. The bazaars on the Silk Route would have an enormous variety of goods for sale including cotton and silk, farm goods, brassware and porcelain, teas and spices, fruits, vegetables, tobacco and opium, dyes and cosmetics.

The beautifully embroidered cap shown here appears to have been made in the mid-nineteenth century. It is in a very new condition and does not appear to have been worn; possibly it was made as a special gift for a wedding, or some other celebration. The cap is made in a rich red quilted silk with brightly coloured stitching, and is lined with plain cotton, apart from the bottom band which has a red printed cotton lining.

It is worked entirely in corded quilting except for the lower border, the cords being inserted during the working process and held in position by lines of running stitch. The cap is made in eight sections and is in such a pristine condition that it was impossible to find exactly where the joins of the sections are. In

(above) *The front of the tabard showing the motifs in satin stitch. Designed and worked by Maureen Pallister* (PHOTOGRAPHY: PETER WRIGHT)

(left) *Chinese Turkestan cap in red silk, lined with plain and printed cotton. It is almost entirely cord-quilted, with lines of running stitch holding the cords in position, embroidered in satin stitch with floss silks (purple, turquoise, yellow and white) EG no 33 1983; height 14cm (5¹/₂in), base diameter 17cm (6³/₄in), circumference 47cm (18¹/₂in)* (PHOTOGRAPHY: DUDLEY MOSS)

A sample showing Italian quilting on fine needle cord. Designed and worked by Maureen Pallister (PHOTOGRAPHY: PETER WRIGHT)

Map showing position of the Silk Route

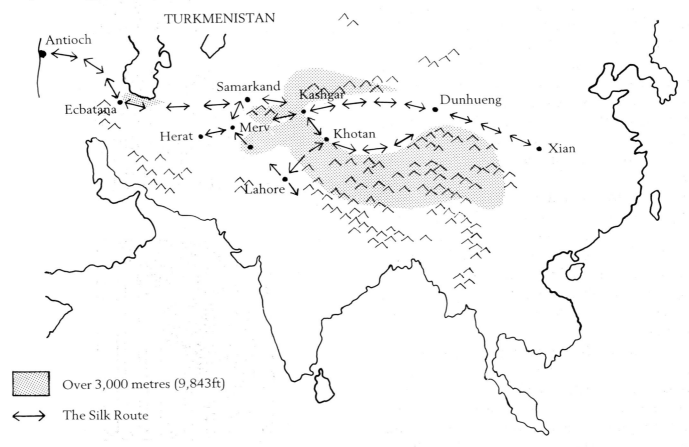

TURKMENISTAN

Antioch

Ecbatana

Samarkand

Kashgar

Dunhueng

Herat

Merv

Khotan

Xian

Lahore

[dotted key] Over 3,000 metres (9,843ft)

⟷ The Silk Route

most sections there are twelve quilted channels, except for three sections which have thirteen channels.

At first sight the corded quilting appears wrapped or satin stitched, but closer examination reveals that the quilting stitches are threaded back and forth with the silk, so none of the precious thread is wasted inside the cap. The geometric patterns are worked in brightly coloured floss silks using shades of purple, turquoise, yellow and white. These patterns were often symbolic, and the turquoise, yellow and white stitching is thought to represent insects or lizards. Each compartment is outlined with spaced buttonhole stitch in white cotton. The lower border has black threads taken from the front to the inside, and black cotton chain stitch is worked on the surface not through the fabric. There are seven black rows, with a blue row at the top and bottom giving the appearance of a strip of knitting. It is decorated with cross stitch in horizontal 'S' motifs using a white cotton thread.

Even after close examination it is impossible to state with certainty how the corded quilting was worked. The method most commonly used threads cords through stitched channels, but this does not seem possible here, as there is no sign of any entry or exit for the cords, and threading up to a point and back could not be done without coming through the lining fabric and going back in again. Several experiments were made to emulate the intricate work on the cap, and the only technique which achieved a similar effect was a line of running stitches through two layers of fabric, with a cord between the two fabrics parallel to the stitching and then another row close to the cord.

The cap may have been made for sale, as many items were from the mid-nineteenth century. Hats characterised male tribal dress and the owner's status was indicated by the richness of the fabric and embroidery (that is, the use of silk, cotton, gold and silver). Originally, patterns may have indicated a particular region, but it is no longer possible to be certain of this as patterns are subject to changes in fashion and the movement of nomadic people. Red is the preferred colour of the Turkmen and much used in embroidery and woven fabrics. There are many references to red in the songs and poetry of the region, particularly speaking of marriage and birth. Madder was widely cultivated in Turkestan and was the cheapest source of the red dye colour. Kermes (an insect on the evergreen oak) and cochineal were also used.

Many articles from this area were lined with brightly printed cottons, and although there is some evidence of the manufacture of these cottons in Turkestan, the fabric used to line this particular hat was most probably imported from India or from Russia. During the early 1800s, cheap Russian cotton prints were beginning to supplant the traditional Turkestan textiles.

The closely stitched lines of quilting on the cap make a very strong, firm fabric and this suggests garments used for protection, such as those worn under armour. The quilting is also reminiscent of the exquisite wrappings and bindings found on Japanese Samurai armour. This combination of a military theme with the corded quilting on the cap inspired the contemporary piece shown here. I made a series of small experiments with corded quilting on a variety of fabrics, including silks, velvet and fine needlecord. Decoration was added in bands of satin stitches in coloured threads. The idea of making garments arose from the working of these samples. A tabard is both a comfort and a protection and seemed an ideal choice, combining the two themes of armour and quilting. Several commercial patterns are available for tabards, waistcoats or body warmers which could be used in this way.

I chose a fine dark purple needlecord for the tabard, and a printed cotton for the lining. Black fleecy domette, sometimes called icewool, was used as padding as it is more flexible for clothes than polyester or terylene wadding, and one or two layers can be used, depending on the thickness of the fabric.

Using a matching thread, the channels were machine-stitched in flowing vertical lines echoing the curved shape of the tabard. Extra decoration was

a)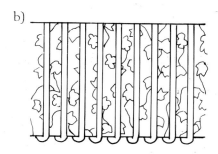

b)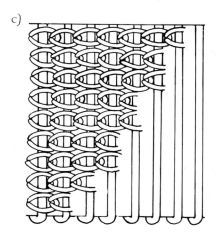

c)

d)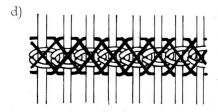

Stitch diagrams

a) *Floss silk laced through running stitches of quilted channels*
b) *Black cotton thread over lower border of card or felt*
c) *Raised or detached chain stitch over bars*
d) *Cross stitch over chain stitch (lower border)*

(DRAWINGS: MOLLIE PICKEN)

added in the form of stylised motifs forming a V-shape at the neck. These were hand-stitched in silk threads in purple, burnt orange, dark red and beige. Just as the Turkestan cap was designed for everyday wear, the contemporary tabard makes a comfortable as well as a decorative garment for practical use.

INDEX